Rembrandt
under the scalpel

The Anatomy Lesson of Dr Nicolaes Tulp Dissected

This catalogue accompanies the exhibition

Rembrandt under the Scalpel.
The Anatomy Lesson of Dr Nicolaes Tulp Dissected

in the Mauritshuis, The Hague
3 October 1998 - 10 January 1999

Rembrandt
under the scalpel

The Anatomy Lesson of Dr Nicolaes Tulp Dissected

Norbert Middelkoop

Petria Noble

Jørgen Wadum

Ben Broos

Mauritshuis, The Hague

Six Art Promotion bv, Amsterdam

CIP information
ISBN 90-71056-12-0
(ISBN 90-7156-11-2 Dutch edition)
© 1998, Six Art Promotion bv, Amsterdam
        Mauritshuis, The Hague
Authors: B. Broos, N.E. Middelkoop, P. Noble and J. Wadum

Index

Preface

On 26 June 1817, Cornelis Apostool, director of the Rijksmuseum in Amsterdam, wrote a letter to the commissioner of the Ministry of Education, Arts and Sciences drawing attention to the lamentable condition of Rembrandt's *Anatomy Lesson of Dr Nicolaes Tulp*. At that time, the painting was hanging in the Waag (Weighhouse), the former quarters of the Amsterdam Surgeons' Guild, which was disbanded by the French in 1798. The circumstances there were far from ideal. Shortly before, it had even been ascertained that due to leaks 'almost the entire canvas had been damaged by rot' and that the paint was threatening to fall off. Concerted efforts saved the painting, at least temporarily, but Apostool thought that it deserved to hang in a museum. For the time being, however, his plea fell on deaf ears.

The situation changed only ten years later, in 1828, when the administrators of the Surgeons' Widows Fund decided to sell the painting at auction. This time, the State (seated in The Hague) was interested, and a few weeks prior to the auction the public sale of the painting was forbidden by Royal Decree. The painting's estimated value of 32,000 guilders was beyond the means of the City of Amsterdam and it was consequently purchased by the State. For Apostool, who had initiated the entire matter in 1817, the disappointment must have been great indeed when King Willem I subsequently allotted the painting to 'his' Royal Cabinet in The Hague, or the Mauritshuis.

Since then, Rembrandt's group portrait has remained one of the cornerstones of the museum's collection. The painting is most frequently complimented for its maker's ingenious solution to a very complicated commission: namely the portrayal of eight gentlemen in a composition that is neither boring nor monotonous. The importance of Rembrandt's work, however, only becomes clear when it is examined within the tradition of the series of Amsterdam anatomy-lesson pictures, which began in 1603 with the *Anatomy Lesson of Dr Sebastiaen Egbertsz* by Aert Pietersz and extended well into the eighteenth century. Hence, it has been a long fostered wish to surround 'Tulp' with a selection of the other Amsterdam 'anatomy lessons'. The completion of the painting's restoration provided the ideal opportunity for this plan. And, the collaboration with the Amsterdams Historisch Museum, which was prepared to lend four of its loveliest anatomy-lesson paintings, fulfilled this wish.

The exhibition consists of three parts. The first part focuses on the scenes of anatomy lessons, enhanced with a selection of medical instruments used for these lessons as well as archival material. The second part highlights the person of Nicolaes Tulp and was made possible thanks to a number of important loans from the Six Collection in Amsterdam. The final part documents the restorers' treatment of the *Anatomy Lesson of Dr Nicolaes Tulp*.

As always, many individuals contributed to the realisation of the exhibition and the catalogue. The essay on the art collection of the Amsterdam Surgeons' Guild was written by Norbert Middelkoop, curator at the Amsterdams Historisch Museum. In it, the art-historical, social and medical aspects of this genre are explored. Ben Broos and Jørgen Wadum co-authored the essay on the history of the restoration of the *Anatomy Lesson of Dr Nicolaes Tulp*. They relied on archival material as well as what can still be deduced from the condition of the painting itself. The report on the recently completed restoration was compiled by Petria Noble and Jørgen Wadum, who were responsible for the actual restoration. Marguerite Stuart also worked on the exhibition as an intern. Coordination of the exhibition and the accompanying publication were the responsibility of Peter van der Ploeg and Marlies Enklaar.

Technical research for the restoration would not have been possible without the generous assistance of Klaas Jan van der Berg, Karin Groen, Muriel Geldof, Susan de Groot, Peter Hallebeek, Ron Heeren, Henk van Keulen, Sandra Kemp and Kees Mensch. For advice, we could always turn to Martin Bijl, David Bomford, Lesley Carlyle, Mireille te Marvelde, Alan Phenix and Ernst van de Wetering.

Our countless questions with respect to the medical aspects were graciously answered by
Dr B. Baljet (Anatomical-Embryological Department of the Academic Medical Centre, University
of Amsterdam) and Prof. Dr H. Beukers (Leiden State University). We should also like to thank
A.J.F. Gogelein,
Drs C. de Graaf (Archive, Leiden) and K.S. Grooss (Boerhaave Museum, Leiden) for their time.
The exhibition could not have taken place without the unique loans from the Amsterdams Historisch
Museum and the Six Collection in Amsterdam. We are therefore deeply indebted to Pauline
Kruseman and Jhr J. Six. Other loans were kindly made available by the Boerhave Museum in Leiden
and the Gemeentearchief Amsterdam (Municipal Archive).

The time-consuming and costly restoration of the *Anatomy Lesson of Dr Nicolaes Tulp* and the
exhibition was made possible in part by a generous contribution from Akzo Nobel and Organon
respectively on the occasion of Organon's 75th anniversary. I should like to extend a special word
of thanks to Mr C.J.A. van Lede and Mr T. Kalff and their assistants for their enormous support and
enthusiasm.

The Mauritshuis is grateful that it could once again realise a special project with the support of
so many wonderful colleagues and friends from its own circle as well as from the business community.
This makes clear that concern for the preservation and optimal presentation of our cultural heritage
resonates far and wide.

Frederik J. Duparc
Director

I 'Large and magnificent Paintings, all pertaining to the Chirurgeon's Art'. The Art Collection of the Amsterdam Surgeons' Guild

Norbert E. Middelkoop

Despite all hardships – fire, neglect, 'restoration' and sale – the collection of paintings of the Amsterdam Surgeons' Guild has remained more or less intact up to the present day,[1] the majority of the paintings being kept in the Amsterdams Historisch Museum.[2] In its origins and history the collection may justly be termed unique: in the seventeenth and eighteenth centuries there is no other example of a single institution being responsible for a regular succession of mutually comparable commissions over a long period of time. In the present article I shall explore the collection in chronological order. The chief sources for this are the Guild's archives, now kept in the Municipal Archives of Amsterdam, and an eighteenth-century manuscript by the surgeon Johannes Monnikhoff, who copied parts of archival documents which have since been lost.[3] Although naturally enough the bulk of the paintings discussed here are anatomy pieces, I shall also pay attention to the group portraits in which no anatomy lesson is taking place. As far as the surgeons themselves were concerned, the two types were inextricably interwoven.[4]

1. Aert Pietersz
The Anatomy Lesson of Dr Sebastiaen Egbertsz,
1601-1603
Canvas, 147 x 392 cm
Amsterdams Historisch
Museum, inv. no. A 7387

Anatomy Lessons and Anatomy Pieces

On a cursory viewing of Aert Pietersz's *Anatomy Lesson of Dr Sebastiaen Egbertsz* of 1603 one might be forgiven for thinking that this was one of those early civic-guard paintings in which the painter was faced with the task of giving every militiaman equal prominence in the painting (fig. 1). Grateful use was made of the table as a space-creating compositional device. Where otherwise one might expect to see the festive spread, however, here there is a corpse – and the cutlery that some of those present seem to have brought with them turns out on closer inspection to be medical instruments for the purpose of dissecting the *subjectum anatomicum*. This is no civic-guard piece, then, even if Aert Pietersz did employ the skills of that related genre: it is an anatomy piece, the painted representation of an anatomy lesson by a *doctor medicinae* in the presence of a group of surgeons.

When Aert Pietersz (*c.* 1550-1612) painted the *Anatomy Lesson of Dr Sebastiaen Egbertsz* between 1601 and 1603 – it is the earliest known Dutch painting of a dissection – the Amsterdam Guild of Surgeons was half a century old.[5] In 1552 it had broken away from the craft of slipper-makers, clog-makers and skate-makers. Three years later the Guild was given permission every year to dissect the body of an executed criminal for the purpose of teaching anatomy. Initially these dissections took place in the convent of St Ursula, but following the Alteration of 1578, as a result of which the monastic orders were disbanded and their buildings confiscated by the Protestant city government, the surgeons were given a room in the chapel of the former convent of St Margaret on the Nes (fig. 2). The Surgeons' Guild shared the floor with two chambers of rhetoric; on the ground floor there was a meat market. Burgomaster Marten Jansz Coster (*c.* 1510-1594) was elected the first *praelector anatomiae*: reader or prelector in anatomy.

2. Claes Jansz. Visscher
The Large and Small Meat Hall on the Nes, 1611
Amsterdam,
Gemeentearchief

In the seventeenth century a surgeon (or 'chirurgeon') was first and foremost a craftsman, albeit that his activities related to the human body. Master surgeons were authorized to treat external complaints and carry out operations, often practising their trade in little shops where the citizen could have himself examined (fig. 3).[6] The most common of these procedures was having one's hair cut, which is why barbers were also affiliated to the Surgeons' Guild. To prevent unfair competition and quackery the surgeons' rights and obligations were defined in by-laws and ordinances. Thus the by-law of 1597 contains instructions for the administration of the master's examination by two examiners from the Guild's college of wardens, while the *Ordinance on Anatomy* of 1606 lays down the details of the anatomical training to be given to surgeons, assistants and apprentices.[7]

The prelector who did the teaching was appointed by the city from among the *medicinae doctores*: qualified doctors of medicine whose principal field was the treatment of disease. Twice a week he would teach osteology, physiology, surgery and zoology.

The public lessons in anatomy given by the prelector were organized by the guild. Usually each lesson would take more than a day, and they were held in winter as the corpse remained in good condition longer when temperatures were low. These lessons were open not only to members of the guild but also to outsiders. Although originally established for scientific purposes, by about the end of the sixteenth century the public dissection had grown into a popular event for the citizenry.[8] In 1593 a *Theatrum Anatomicum* was built specially for the purpose in Leiden. Even when no anatomy lesson was in progress it was possible – for a fee – to view the unusual interior. An engraving of 1609 shows human and animal skeletons set up on the tiers in the circular gallery (fig. 4). Moralizing maxims remind the visitor of the ephemerality of existence. In a suitable context of this kind the dissection of a human cadaver was justifiable: the soul of the executed criminal – invariably from another town – was now, after all, beyond redemption.

3. Egbert van Heemskerck
The Surgeon Jacob Hercules in his shop, 1669
Canvas, 70 x 59 cm
Amsterdams Historisch
Museum, inv. no. A 2121

In Amsterdam it was to be 1691 before the surgeons had their own large *Theatrum Anatomicum*. Little is known about the interior of the earlier dissection rooms, let alone the question of whether there as in Leiden there was so much emphasis on the *memento mori* message. From the adapted version of a poem written by Caspar Barlaeus (1584-1648) in 1639 on the occasion of the opening of the dissection room in the Kleine Vleeshal (Small Meat Hall) – the former St Margaret's Chapel – one has first and foremost an impression of the scientific importance that was attached to dissecting the mortal remains of sinners. They served to enrich our knowledge of health and life. The lesson that was appended to this was that God resides in even the smallest part of the human body:

> Wrongdoers, harmful to the human race,
> Still serve a purpose when they are put to death.
> Surgery seeks out good, even from death.
> The speechless skeleton teaches. Even the dead limbs
> Advise us that we must avoid such shame,
> Head, brain, tongue, heart, lung, kidney, bones, finger, hand,
> They all can serve to instruct the living.
> Listener, learn from this to discover yourself,
> And while you attend to everything, hold this for certain
> That God's power is hidden in the slightest part.[9]

That public dissections were popular events in the life of Amsterdam is clear from the guild's *Anatomieboek*, a record begun in about 1645, in which are listed the public dissections organized by the guild between 1631 and 1731.[10] Although nothing is known about the numbers attending anatomy lessons in the early years, from the details of receipts from the later demonstrations it may be deduced that these events lasting several days must have been followed by many hundreds of spectators.[11] An engraving by Andries Stock of about 1615 gives an impression of the level of public

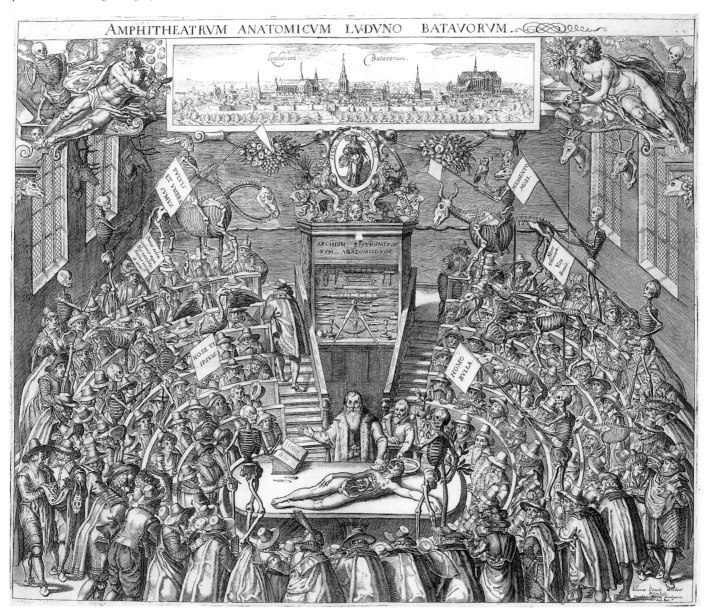

interest and the crowd during an anatomy lesson (fig. 5). Although this scene is usually interpreted as an anatomy lesson given in Leiden by the anatomist Pieter Pauw (1564-1617), the situation depicted is closely similar to what one might have expected to find in the Kleine Vleeshal in Amsterdam in about 1615.[12]

4. Bartholomeus Dolendo after Jan Cornelisz Woudanus
The Theatrum Anatomicum in Leiden, 1609
Engraving,
46.6 x 55.8 cm
Amsterdam,
Rijksmuseum,
Rijksprentenkabinet

11

5. Andries Stock after
Jacques de Gheyn II
Anatomy Lesson, 1615 (?)
Engraving,
29,4 x 22,9 cm
Amsterdam,
Rijksmuseum,
Rijksprentenkabinet

Sebastiaen Egbertsz and the Earliest Anatomy Pieces

Back to Aert Pietersz. In his *Anatomy Lesson of Dr Sebastiaen Egbertsz* of 1603 (fig. 1) the central
feature of the composition is the body of a man lying on the dissection table. Behind the table stands
Sebastiaen Egbertsz (1563-1621), who became the second prelector of the Surgeons' Guild in 1595.
To judge by the pincers he is holding up, he seems to be pictured at the very beginning of the
dissection. Aert Pietersz may have owed this commission from the surgeons to a civic-guard piece
which he had completed in 1599. This shows the senior officers of a company of civic guards,
standing in two rows one behind the other – at this time already no longer a particularly innovative
approach.[13] What attracted the surgeons must have been the prospect of each individual portrait being
given more or less equal prominence on the canvas, and as observed above the end result looks very
much like a variation of a civic guard banquet. In the same way that we see in the evolution of the
group portrait, this *Anatomy Lesson* testifies to the great desire on the part of those portrayed to be
shown as prominently and clearly as possible – in this case in three-quarter profile. According to notes

by Johannes Monnikhoff, when the painting was completed in 1603 five master surgeons had already died as a result of the plague epidemic of the previous year.[14] Above the surgeons' heads, as was customary, there are numbers by which to identify them. The man on the extreme right holds up a list with the corresponding names from which we can see that all 28 master surgeons of the time are portrayed.[15]

We have no information about the identity of the person whose body served as the *subjectum anatomicum*. However, it would be no surprise if Aert Pietersz had recorded only a fictitious dissection. The original decision to place a dissection at the centre of the picture would have been informed principally by the knowledge that this theme offered the perfect opportunity to depict both the prelector and the surgeons in a group portrait. Sebastiaen Egbertsz's status is accentuated by his prominence in the scene: he is the only standing figure in the middle of the picture who can be seen down to hip height. The instruments that some of those present have with them indicate that they too possess dissection skills. One of the surgeons is holding a shaving bowl, a reference to professional tasks as a barber. The general equality of those portrayed justifies the conclusion that Aert Pietersz was commissioned to paint the picture by the Surgeons' Guild itself, with a modest leading role being accorded to the prelector.

In 1606, three years after the painting was completed, Sebastiaen Egbertsz was elected burgomaster of Amsterdam. His political career proceeded well until 1618, when he was removed from the city council by Stadtholder Maurice of Nassau. As a doctor he continued to run a flourishing practice, however, and in 1619, shortly before his death and 34 years after his elevation to the title of *doctor medicinae*, he saw the Surgeons' Guild move to the Sint-Anthoniswaag. This former gate to the city had been converted into a weigh-house only two years previously, after which the rooms on the upper floors had been made available to various organizations (fig. 6). On 19 April 1619 the prelector officially inaugurated the new room with a lecture on Cornelius Celsus's vision of surgery.[16]

It may well have been to mark the move in 1619 that a second group portrait centred on Sebastiaen Egbertsz was painted (fig. 7). When it was finished later that same year this was hung on

6. Nicolaes Visscher after Simon de Vries
The Weigh-House seen from the Gelderse Kade, early 17th c.
Etching, 16.7 x 21 cm
Amsterdams Historisch Museum, inv. no. A 24770

7. Thomas de Keyser (?)
The Osteology Lesson of Dr Sebastiaen Egbertsz, 1619
Canvas, 135 x 186 cm
Amsterdams Historisch Museum, inv. no. A 7352

the chimney-breast of the new guild chamber.[17] This time the subject was not a dissection but an osteology demonstration – osteology being the study of the human skeleton. Compared with Aert Pietersz's group portrait, this new painting is something of a revolution. Instead of all the master surgeons, now only six persons are portrayed.[18] The list of names at top left allows us to identify those present, and it is striking that, with the exception of the prelector, in 1619 they were all either wardens or examiners of the Guild. The only warden not to appear in this new painting, Albert Jansz Scherm, had been portrayed in 1603.[19] Evidently the initiative for this commission came from the board itself. The absence of the warden who had already been painted before suggests that the surgeons paid for their own portraits – perhaps with the exception of the prelector. The decision to portray only the wardens and the prelector may have been prompted by the intended location for the painting on the chimney breast, which would have been impossible for a painting of larger dimensions.

The traditional requirement of equal prominence for those commissioning the picture has in no way prevented the painter from arriving at a highly original composition. Indeed, it seems to have acted as a stimulus. Four of the subjects are engrossed in the skeleton, which serves as the central element in the composition. In contrast to the painting of 1603, only the two surgeons at the front look out of the picture, though with no slackening of their concentration on the osteology lesson. They act as the element linking the spectator and the scene. The prelector, standing to the left of the skeleton, is wholly absorbed in his teaching and is pointing to the bottom rib. The painter has distinguished him from the other subjects by showing him as the only one wearing a hat. This symbol of his status is subtly underlined by the two surgeons standing on the right and their seated colleague on the left, each of whom holds his hat in his hand. The skeleton, which is depicted with great accuracy and considerable detail, was probably painted from the life – if that is not an inappropriate expression – and is thought to be that of an executed English pirate whose corpse had been made available to the guild in 1615, after which it had been dissected by the prelector himself.[20] Certainly the fact that the skullcap has clearly been removed and subsequently reattached suggests that the skeleton must already have seen some service in the teaching of dissection prior to the demonstration seen here. Attempts to arrive at a symbolical interpretation of this painting – the skeleton being seen as a *vanitas* symbol,[21] – are refuted by the absence of any more explicit references to the transience of mortal life.

In recent years the traditional ascription of this painting to Thomas de Keyser (1596/97-1667) has been called into question. True, Monnikhoff's manuscript refers to 'Thomas de Kijzer' as the painter, but it has recently been suggested that in stylistic terms the picture is more reminiscent of the early work of Nicolaes Eliasz Pickenoy (1590/91-1654/56). Werner van den Valckert (c. 1585-after 1655) is another name that has been put forward.[22] For the time being, the possibility of an attribution to the experienced Van den Valckert looks more attractive than one to De Keyser or Pickenoy, both of whom in 1619 were still at the beginning of their careers – particularly as regards group portraits.[23] Even so, it is as well to be cautious, since Monnikhoff is generally considered reliable and he invariably refers to his own seventeenth-century source. If the piece is not by De Keyser, then at least the confusion dates back to the seventeenth century.[24] On the other hand, if the 1619 *Osteology Lesson* was painted by Pickenoy this would make him the only painter – before Rembrandt, that is – to receive two successive commissions for the painting of anatomy lessons.

Johan Fonteijn: Prelector without Dissection

Sebastiaen Egbertsz died in 1621. He was succeeded in the same year by Dr Johan Fonteijn (1574-1628), the following milestone in whose career was his appointment in 1623 to be personal physician to Maurice of Nassau. Although as a medical man and a lover of the arts and sciences he enjoyed the respect of his contemporaries – among them Vondel and Tulp – little is known of his achievements at the dissecting table.[25] It is possible that it was on their account that in the early 1620s the surgeons began to feel the need for improved facilities for their public dissections. In February 1624 a small panelled anatomical theatre after the Leiden example was built inside the guild chamber in the old weigh-house (cf. fig. 4). This was followed, a year later, by a tightening up of both the rules and the admission charges for spectators at anatomy lessons.[26] It is possible that the new fitting out of the guild's dissection theatre played a part in the initiative to have the next group portrait painted. This was to commemorate Fonteijn's work as prelector.

According to Monnikhoff's source, on 6 September 1625 Nicolaes Eliasz Pickenoy received 'from the Wardens and the eldest of the guild' the commission to paint a portrait of Fonteijn and ten surgeons. The commission was probably issued after the annual transfer of control to the new board, an event which generally took place in September.[27] From the surviving list of names it is possible to deduce that at least the two new wardens were included in the picture: the other wardens and examiners who were kept their seats on the board had already had their portraits painted in 1603 or 1619 (figs 1 and 7).[28] Apart from the wardens, the picture shows eight surgeons of whom six were past guild assistants. With one exception, in 1625 none of them had previously served as a warden.[29]

The choice of a combination of two wardens, six guild assistants and two surgeons may to some extent have been informed by the practical circumstance that it was precisely 'the Wardens and the eldest of the guild' who already, for the most part at least, had their portraits hanging in the guild chamber. The tendency to bring mainly the younger members together in a group portrait round the prelector was to continue in subsequent paintings of anatomy lessons. The date given for this particular commission, 6 September 1625, makes it extremely unlikely that the *Anatomy Lesson of Dr Johan Fonteijn* is linked to any particular public dissection, since as we have already seen these were held during the winter. It seems, incidentally, that Pickenoy found executing this commission more than a little troublesome: 'This piece having been in hand for more than a whole year, and in the meantime Arend Allertsz having died after sitting only once, it was finally finished and taken to the Guild Chamber on the 15th of October 1626.'[30]

Sadly, precisely what the picture looked like at this time cannot now be determined. In 1723 the canvas was seriously damaged in a fire in the antechamber of the same guild chamber in the Anthoniswaag, four of the figures being lost.[31] During its restoration by Jan Maurits Quinkhard in 1732 the damaged painting was probably substantially trimmed to make it presentable again. Only the top of the painting with the remaining seven portraits, including that of Fonteijn, was preserved (fig. 8). From his pose it is clear that he is in the process of explaining something to the surgeons. The head at top left was originally somewhere else in the painting.[32]

8. Nicolaes Eliasz Pickenoy
The Anatomy Lesson of Dr Johan Fonteijn, 1625-1626 (fragment)
Canvas, 97.5 x 192 cm
Amsterdams Historisch Museum, inv. no. A 2048

We can also only guess at the nature of the dissection procedure that was originally depicted, as research has shown that the table and skull were added later, most probably during the restoration of 1732. It would also have been interesting to know whether the prelector is portrayed during the dissection itself or at some stage immediately preceding it, and to what extent the corpse would have been visible – was there little more than a vague indication of it, as in Aert Pietersz's painting, or could the whole of it be seen? The many unresolved questions are an invitation to attempt a reconstruction of Pickenoy's original composition, especially as in chronological terms it was painted immediately before the famous *Anatomy lesson of Dr Tulp* of 1632 and must therefore have been one of the young Rembrandt's most important sources of inspiration.[33] The height of the canvas can be reconstructed from the height of the horizontal seam joining what were probably the only two strips of canvas on which the picture was painted. This seam is on a level with the bottom edge of the ruff worn by the man at the bottom left of the picture.[34] If we double the height of the upper strip of canvas, which is more or less intact, we arrive at an overall height for the painting of approx. 160 cm.[35] This would mean enough room in the bottom half of the picture for a *subjectum anatomicum*.

9. Michiel and
Pieter van Mierevelt
*The Anatomy Lesson of
Dr Willem van der Meer*,
1617
Canvas, 144 x 198 cm
Delft, Stedelijk Museum
Het Prinsenhof,
inv. no. B 112
(on loan from the
Oude en Nieuwe
Gasthuis, Delft)

>> 11. *The Anatomy Lesson
of Dr Fonteijn*, attempt at
reconstruction by the
author in collaboration
with Thijs Wolzak

This brings us to an earlier successful *Anatomy Lesson* which Pickenoy may have known: the *Anatomy Lesson of Dr Willem van der Meer*, painted in 1617 for the Surgeons' Guild in Delft (fig. 9). The broad outline of this painting was done by the renowned portrait painter Michiel van Mierevelt and further elaborated by his son Pieter. Without going into detail on the subject of the quality of this group portrait, it is fair to say that its composition is reminiscent of the Amsterdam anatomy lesson of 1603 (fig. 1), while the placing of the surgeons and their varying concentration on the lesson or on the spectator anticipates that of 1619 (fig. 7).[36] The action of the Delft prelector looks as if it might follow from that of Sebastiaen Egbertsz in Aert Pietersz's densely populated *Anatomy Lesson*. Here the dissection has just begun: Van der Meer has opened up the abdomen of the prominently placed subject in order to begin by dissecting and removing the more perishable viscera.

Apart from this painting it will also be pertinent at this point to look at an anonymous drawing which may go back to a lost original from the same period as Pickenoy's painting (fig. 10). It shows a dissection of the brain in which, as in the Delft piece, the *subjectum* is conspicuously present and two *repoussoir* figures in the foreground direct the spectator's attention to the action round the dissecting table. Although an origin in Amsterdam does not appear likely, the composition of the drawing may be used as an aid in reconstructing the *Anatomy Lesson of Dr Johan Fonteijn*.[37] The *subjectum anatomicum* has been borrowed from Mierevelt, as has the disposition of the surgeons in front of the dissecting table. These serve the same *repoussoir* function as the two surgeons on either side of the skeleton in the *Osteology Lesson of Dr Sebastiaen Egbertsz* of 1619 (fig. 7), from which, likewise, elements have been borrowed.[38] Judging by the tentative reconstruction of Pickenoy's creation, consisting of ten persons and a prelector (fig. 11), Rembrandt's *Anatomy Lesson of Dr Tulp* may have been less far removed from the earlier anatomy pieces than has hitherto been supposed.

16

10. Unknown artist
An Anatomy Lesson
Drawing
New Haven (Conn.), Yale
University Medical
Library, Clemence Fry
Collection

Nicolaes Tulp and the Lessons of Anatomy

Since the degree to which in 1632 the young Rembrandt (1606-1669) drew inspiration from
Pickenoy's example is something that cannot be even remotely established, in the literature his
Anatomy Lesson of Dr Nicolaes Tulp (fig. 12) has come to occupy an isolated position among the other
anatomy pieces of the Surgeons' Guild. Of course, this is due principally to the master himself, since
the painting marks in conspicuous fashion Rembrandt's arrival on the Amsterdam scene.[39]

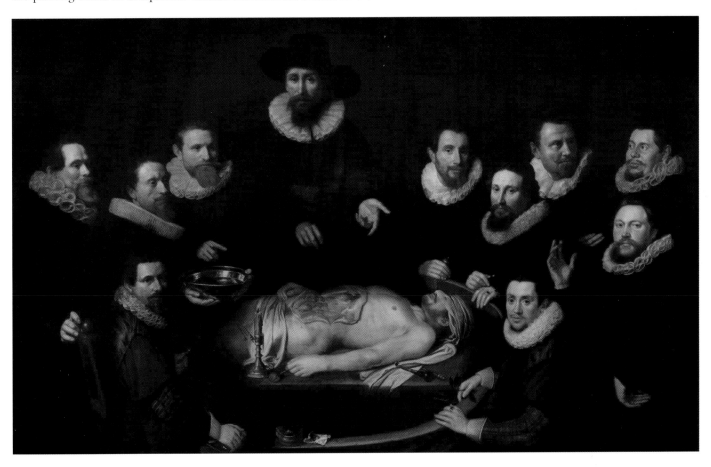

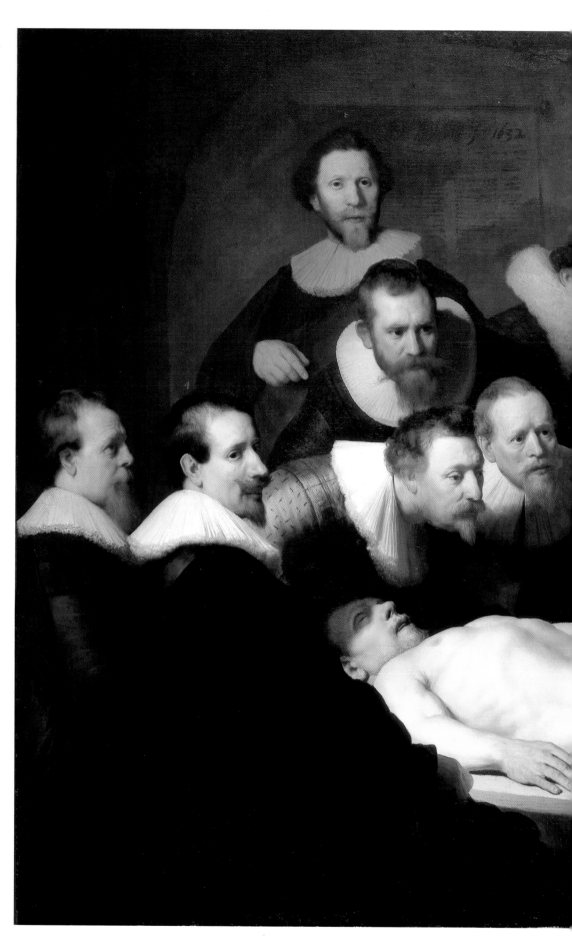

12. Rembrandt
*The Anatomy Lesson of
Dr Nicolaes Tulp*, 1632
Canvas, 169.5 x 216.5 cm
The Hague, Mauritshuis,
inv. no. 146

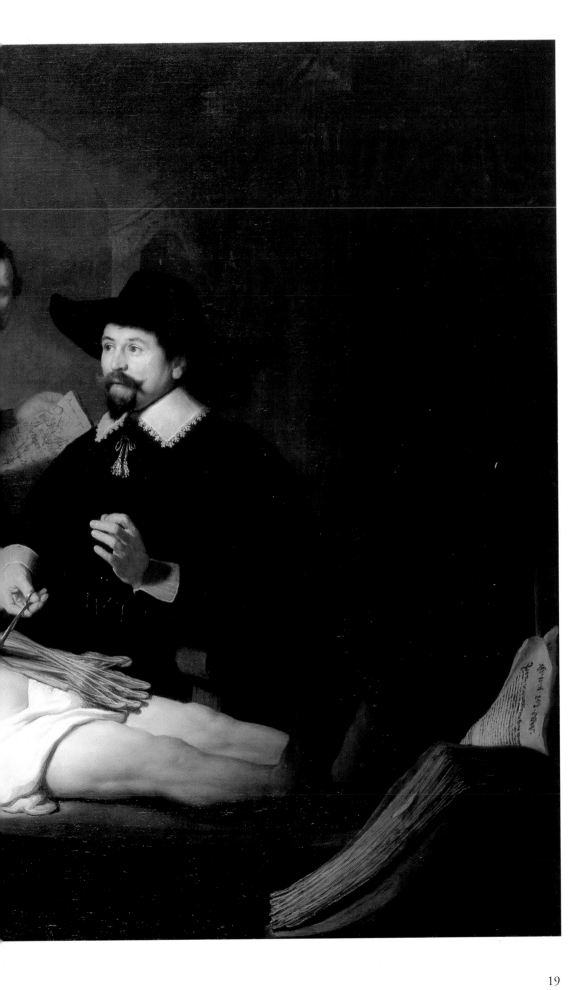

The somewhat diagonal placing of the *subjectum* relative to the picture plane is without precedent in an anatomy piece.[40] Rembrandt proceeded to combine this space-creating device with the careful disposition of the simultaneously lecturing and demonstrating prelector Tulp, who is isolated on one side of the composition both two-dimensionally and three-dimensionally. Tulp's audience, gathered together on the left-hand side of the canvas, are certainly no less prominently present. The stepped positions of the surgeons is a reference to the ring-shaped tiers that might be expected in an anatomy theatre, though without the space being further defined.[41] The sophisticated interplay of light and dark invites the spectator to advance from the shadow and take up position at the dissecting table. The interaction between the anatomy lesson and the spectator is the central theme in two pioneering art-historical studies of the painting, the first by William Hekscher (1958), the second by William Schupbach (1982), and it is with the help of their insights that I shall look briefly at the present state of the research in what follows.[42]

Rembrandt appears at first sight to be presenting us with a realistic representation of an anatomy lesson. For the first time we see a prelector actually engaged in the process of dissection. Seated at the dissecting table, Nicolaes Tulp dissects the lower arm of a *subjectum anatomicum*, addressing his audience as he does so. To the modern spectator the involvement of the others portrayed further reinforces the sense of reality: the surgeons give all their attention to the demonstration, not to the painter as in earlier anatomy pieces. In the direction of their gaze some, such as Adriaen Slabbraen (left foreground), make the connection between practice – at the dissecting table – and theory: the folio volume open on the lectern in the right foreground.[43] With his gaze and half-pointing gesture the surgeon in the background, Frans van Loenen, invites the spectator to witness Tulp's demonstration. Although there is a similar intermediary gesture in the *Osteology Lesson of Dr Egbertsz* of 1619 (fig. 7), Rembrandt's approach comes across as more sophisticated since Van Loenen's role as intermediary between spectator and image is not at the expense of his involvement with the dissection, which is, after all, taking place in front of him.[44]

There are other matters too which create the impression that Rembrandt's first group portrait is an accurate reflection of reality. Nicolaes Tulp, as the successor to Johan Fonteijn, had been the Guild's *praelector anatomiae* since 1628.[45] His first public anatomy lesson was held in 1631, his second a year later on 31 January 1632 and the days following.[46] It was probably this dissection that prompted Tulp to have himself painted with a group of surgeons in the tradition of his predecessors Sebastiaen Egbertsz and Johan Fonteijn. The great difference, then, is that the *Anatomy Lesson of Dr Tulp*, unlike the earlier paintings, can be linked to a documented historical event. Not only are the names of those portrayed known, but also, thanks to the *Anatomieboek* of the Surgeons' Guild, the provenance of the *subjectum anatomicum*: it is supposed to be the corpse of Adriaan Adriaansz, called Het Kint, who on 31 January 1632 was 'punished by the rope on account of his wrongdoing', after which his body was made available to the Guild for dissection.[47] Although the corpse's neck, with its possible traces of the execution, cannot be seen in the picture, and although there is not a single contemporary source to link the name of Het Kint with the cadaver in Rembrandt's painting, it seems reasonable to assume that the painting dated 1632 was executed to commemorate Tulp's public anatomy lesson of that year.[48]

As regards the names of the surgeons seen in the picture we have more to go on: Monnikhoff records them in his manuscript of 1750.[49] Moreover, they were written, for purposes of identification, on the sheet of paper held by Hartman Hartmansz, the surgeon in the right background.[50] At the time of Tulp's anatomy lesson, early in 1632, two of the subjects were wardens of the Guild.[51] According to the *Anatomieboek*, the Guild's four wardens and two examiners were all present at this lesson. The reason for their not all having themselves painted by Rembrandt is again probably the fact that, with one exception, they already appeared in earlier anatomy paintings that hung in the Guild Chamber.[52] The result of this is that in Rembrandt's *Anatomy Lesson* those surgeons who had not previously served as wardens were in the majority,[53] just as had been the case in Pickenoy's painting of 1625-6 (fig. 8).

Yet the *Anatomy Lesson of Dr Tulp* has less to do with the reality of dissection than might be thought at first sight. Good practice laid down that at the beginning of each dissection the prelector should open the abdomen, describe and discuss the fast degenerating organs and then remove them (cf. fig. 9). The fact that in this case the whole process appears instead to have started with the forearm has encouraged many scholars to seek a symbolic interpretation. At the same time, medical historians and anatomists in particular have seized upon a study of the *subjectum* in general and the dissection of the lower arm in particular. For many years a lively debate went on about the supposedly inaccurate representation of the opened-up arm, which was claimed to be due to Rembrandt's erroneous interpretation of examples given in anatomical textbooks.[54] In many cases these studies overlooked the question of whether Tulp and the surgeons would have been likely to

13. After Johann Stephan von Kalkar
Woodcut, 34.8 x 24.3 cm
Frontispiece from Andreas Vesalius, *De humani corporis fabrica libri septem*, Basle 1555
Private collection U.S.A.

accept such a misconception in a painting to be hung in their Guild Chamber.

Today it is generally accepted that Rembrandt is guilty of no anatomical error and that he was working from a prepared arm – prepared, probably, by Tulp.[55] This might also explain the slight discrepancy in the proportions of the left and right arms. The prepared arm was probably 'painted onto' the already completed *subjectum* afterwards. Since the rest of the corpse is intact, the emphasis automatically shifts to the dissection of the forearm. Tulp is using forceps to lift a few muscle bellies connected to the long flexors and tensors of the hand and fingers: the *musculus flexor digitorum superficialis* and the *musculus flexor digitorum profundis*.

14. After Johann Stephan von Kalkar
Portrait of Andreas Vesalius
Woodcut, 19.6 x 14.5 cm
Illustration from Andreas Vesalius, *De humani corporis fabrica libri septem*, Basle 1555 (Private collection U.S.A.)

Hekscher has linked the choice of a dissection of the forearm to the theories of Andreas Vesalius (1514-1564).[56] Vesalius, a medical man originally from Brussels, had more or less abolished the distinction between theory and practice in the teaching of medicine. During his lectures in such cities as Padua, Bologna and Louvain he had himself carried out the anatomical work previously left to an assistant. The title print of Vesalius's *De humani corporis fabrica libri septem* (The Seven Books on the Structure of the Human Body), published in 1543, shows him standing beside the dissecting table in an imaginary anatomy theatre, explaining his theories to a large audience gathered round him (fig. 13). Tulp was familiar with Vesalius's theories from his teacher in Leiden, Pieter Pauw, who had himself been a pupil of Vesalius. It was at Pauw's initiative that the Leiden *Theatrum Anatomicum* (fig. 4) had been built. In *De humani corporis fabrica* Vesalius describes the arm as the physician's chief instrument, the 'primarium medicinae instrumentum',[57] and significantly on the frontispiece he had himself depicted with a prepared forearm (fig. 14). Thus the dissection of the forearm in Rembrandt's group portrait makes of Tulp a new Vesalius, a *Vesalius redivivus*.

Attempts at identifying the large volume on the lectern as Vesalius's *magnum opus* or a later adaptation of it have so far proved unconvincing. The pages in Vesalius that deal with the anatomy of arm and hand have typography different from that of the folio in the painting.[58] Another book that has been suggested as a source, Adriaen van den Spieghel's *De humani corporis fabrica libri decem* of 1627, can be ruled out on the same grounds,[59] even though one of the engravings from that work does show an opened-up arm closely similar to that depicted in the painting. While it is quite possible that Rembrandt studied this and other illustrations, it may be wondered whether it is necessary to identify the volume on the lectern at all. If Tulp had thought it important to be associated with a particular publication, he would unquestionably have ensured that at least it would be possible to recognize the anatomical illustration to be seen on the paper held by Hartman Hartmansz. The extended arm on the sheet (fig. 26 on p. 63) does bear some resemblance to Vesalius's example. In the context of the painting, both sheet and book may be seen as references to the theory against which the practice of anatomy must always be tested. Rembrandt was quite accustomed to using props of this kind to hint at his sitters' erudition.[60]

Following Hekscher's study, in which most of the above aspects of the *Anatomy Lesson of Dr Tulp* had already been discussed, other scholars too developed interesting theories about the painting. Reference has already been made to the series of publications about the dissection of the lower arm. In 1978 the Mauritshuis published the results of an interdisciplinary study of the painting, including much new information about the material history of the canvas.[61] An X-ray photograph showed that Frans van Loenen, the surgeon at the back of the group, was originally painted wearing a hat (see p. 71). It also became clear that the figure of Hartman Hartmansz had originally been higher in the picture area and that the portrait of Jacob Koolvelt, on the extreme left, was added at a late stage. Indeed, his place in the composition was described as unfortunate, a change made after the completion of the painting, possibly even by a painter other than Rembrandt.[62] Encouraged by the new data, in 1982 Schupbach presented a photographic reconstruction of the painting as it would have looked when first painted (fig. 15).

The recently completed restoration of the painting has not only made the anatomical illustration held by Hartman Hartmansz clearer, it has also revealed that both Koolvelt's portrait and Van Loenen's hat are among the alterations that the young Rembrandt made as the job progressed. It has also been established that Jacob de Wit originally bent over forward less far than is now the case. On the basis of this information it is now possible to make a new reconstruction of the *Anatomy Lesson of Dr Tulp* which gives us a snapshot of a stage in Rembrandt's creative process (fig. 43 on p. 70).

Both the Mauritshuis study and Schupbach's reconstruction praise the cohesion of the reduced composition with only six surgeons. Their portraits form two imaginary triangles, a large one with a smaller one within it. The surgeons composing the inner triangle pay close attention to what the prelector is doing; the others are all looking out of the picture. In his attractive interpretation of the painting Schupbach detects several different stages of concentration on what Tulp is doing and saying. Regardless of the tenability or otherwise of his hypothesis about the composition of the painting, Schupbach is right when he observes that the varied ways in which the degree to which Tulp's words are getting through to his audience is depicted is related to what we might expect to see in history painting. In that most respected of all genres of painting, representing both the most important moment in a narrative and the range of emotions that accompany it was a point of honour and one of the greatest challenges facing the artist. The surgeons' moods may thus be linked to Tulp's lecture, which according to this hypothesis has self-evidently reached a climax. The prelector lends weight to his demonstration of the function of the flexors and tensors of arm and hand with a gesture of his left hand – and this is not, therefore, merely the gesture of a man speaking.[63] In this interpretation,

22

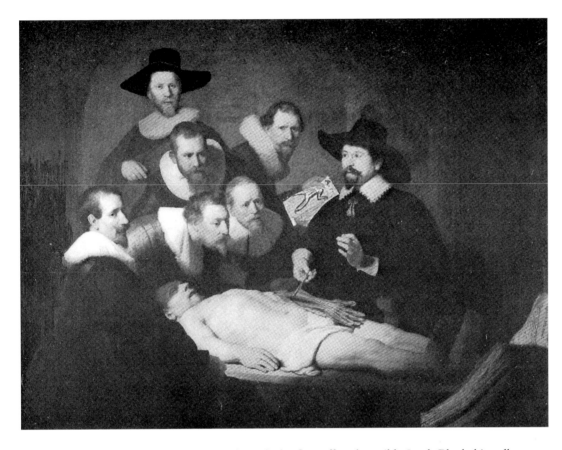

15. William Schupbach, reconstruction of Rembrandt's *Anatomy Lesson of Dr Tulp*, 1982

Matthijs Calkoen, the surgeon next to Tulp with the flat ruff, and possibly Jacob Block, his colleague behind him and to the left of him in the picture, are watching Tulp's bending hand rather than observing his face as had always been assumed.

To lend force to his interpretation, Schupbach has tried to discover what words Tulp may have used during his anatomy lesson. To do this he consulted Tulp's master Pieter Pauw and the anatomist Andreas Laurentius (1558-1609).[64] Contemporary accounts of orations and anatomy lessons tell us that the dissection itself was often preceded by a moralistic preamble in which the audience were encouraged to acknowledge their own mortality and it was explained that the science of anatomy was a path towards knowledge of God.[65] It is a message of this kind, Schupbach argues, that is contained in the *Anatomy Lesson of Dr Tulp*. With his dissection the prelector draws the surgeons' attention to the divinity of creation, emphasizing his words by demonstrating the working of the fine mesh of muscles in the arm and hand – the parts of the body regarded by contemporary anatomical literature as the most visible proof of God's presence in man.[66] The successive stages of reaction to Tulp's argument by the surgeons – from silent contemplation to complete assimilation of the message – heighten the drama of the scene. Schupbach believed he could retrieve the text being used by Tulp in the painting from the poem by Barlaeus of 1639, to which reference was made earlier (see p. 10). In particular, the final lines of the first edition apply to the lecturing and demonstrating prelector: 'Here speaks to us the eloquence of learned Tulp as with skilful hand he cuts the pallid limbs'.[67]

According to Schupbach, Tulp's positive view of anatomy has been paradoxically merged with Van Loenen's message to the spectator.[68] By pointing to the body deprived of the soul Van Loenen confronts us with the transience of human existence in the same kind of way as the *memento mori* symbolism of many still-life pieces and portraits.[69] The two supposed meanings of the group portrait are not contradictory: rather, they complement each other. Rembrandt's painting extends the moralistic tenor of the scene to the spectator, who in the very act of being made party to Tulp's demonstration of the divine presence in man has a mirror held up to him.

In 1633, a year after Rembrandt painted the *Anatomy Lesson of Dr Tulp*, Tulp had his portrait painted by Nicolaes Eliasz Pickenoy (fig. 1 on p. 75).[70] The emblematic character of this new work supports the notion that it was very probably the prelector who instructed the young Rembrandt in the execution of the largest commission of his career up to then. But however far we wish to go in our interpretation of Rembrandt's *Anatomy Lesson of Dr Tulp* – ranging from 'a scientific *tableau vivant*'[71] through 'the triumph of *Sapientia* over *Malitia*'[72] to the paradoxical combination of the negative and positive lessons to be learnt from anatomy[73] – comparing it with the earlier *Anatomy*

16. Rembrandt
*The Anatomy Lesson of
Dr Jan Deijman*, 1656
(fragment)
Canvas, 113 x 135 cm
(98.5 x 132.5 cm without
the later additions)
Amsterdams Historisch
Museum, inv. no. A 7394

Lessons of Dr Sebastiaen Egbertsz (figs 1 and 7) and Dr Willem van der Meer (fig. 9) we are forced to conclude that in anatomical terms Rembrandt's group portrait is the furthest removed from reality.[74]

Caspar Barlaeus wrote his poem in 1639 to mark the opening of a new anatomical theatre in the Kleine Vleeshal on the Nes. With the departure of the rhetoricians the Surgeons' Guild was now able to use the whole of the floor above the hall. The first public anatomy lesson in the new room was given by prelector Tulp in the same year as the move.[75] The *Collegium Medicum* or Medical Council established on Tulp's initiative in 1637 also moved into part of the space that had become available. The new board consisted of doctors and apothecaries and was charged with overseeing the health of the city.[76]

Jan Deijman: Prelector without a Head

The exceptional status accorded to the *Anatomy Lesson of Dr Tulp* is further enhanced by the fact that not only the preceding painting by Pickenoy has come down to us in a mutilated condition but also Rembrandt's own *Anatomy Lesson of Dr Jan Deijman*, which came after it (fig. 16). This anatomy piece of 1656 is likewise a fragment of a painting largely destroyed by fire. Jan Deijman (1619-1666) is now known for nothing else but for being the decapitated prelector in Rembrandt's painting, but if things had been only very slightly different even that dubious honour would have escaped him. When in October 1652 Nicolaes Tulp - after eleven documented public anatomy lessons - announced his intention of retiring, the city initially approached the Leiden anatomist Johannes van Horne (1621-1670) for the post of prelector.[77] It was only the intervention of the university of Leiden, which made him a better offer, that kept van Horne where he was and allowed Jan Deijman - as second choice - to succeed Tulp on 27 January 1653.

Deijman's first documented public dissection for the Surgeons' Guild took place three years later and was held in the anatomy theatre of the Kleine Vleeshal.[78] Once again a group portrait was commissioned to commemorate the event, and once again the artist chosen was Rembrandt - clearly the surgeons had been much taken with his previous performance. Perhaps because of the long period that had elapsed since the painting of the *Anatomy Lesson of Dr Tulp*, there was now sufficient demand among the wardens of the guild to have themselves painted again.[79] Originally the painting depicted - besides Jan Deijman, his assistant and the *subjectum anatomicum* - four wardens, one examiner and two other members of the guild.[80] The second examiner, despite having attended Deijman's anatomy lesson in January 1656, declined the honour.[81]

Rembrandt's second anatomy piece was largely destroyed by the fire of 1723, the same conflagration in which Pickenoy's *Anatomy lesson of Dr Fonteijn* fell prey to the flames, but its subsequent restoration may also have contributed to the mutilation of the picture.[82] Seven of the original nine figures in the group were lost. What remains is the anatomical action on the dissecting table. The picture as it exists today is dominated by the corpse of the executed Joris Fonteijn,[83] which came through the fire relatively unharmed. This is in sharp contrast to the fate that befell the prelector: the fire deprived Deijman of his head. The man looking on with the skullcap in his hand has been identified on good grounds as Gijsbert Calkoen, the guild assistant and hence assistant during the anatomy lesson.[84] He was the son of Matthijs Evertsz Calkoen, who is portrayed by Rembrandt in the *Anatomy Lesson of Dr Tulp*. Two hands seen in the fragment to left and right of Calkoen are reminders of the vanished portraits of the other surgeons.

17. Rembrandt
The Anatomy Lesson of Dr Jan Deijman, 1656
Pen and brush in grey and black ink, lightly washed,
110 x 133 mm
Amsterdams Historisch Museum, inv. no. A 7395

18. *The Anatomy Lesson of Dr Deijman*, attempt at reconstruction by the author in collaboration with Thijs Wolzak

A drawing by Rembrandt gives us an impression of what the whole composition would have looked like (fig. 17). The surviving fragment corresponds to the part in the central foreground, and a comparison shows that the original canvas must have been something like 245 by 300 cm in size. Rembrandt had situated his group portrait in a small *theatrum anatomicum*, and in the drawing we can see two tiers of the auditorium surrounding the dissecting table. Those present seem to be looking either at what the prelector is doing or out towards the spectator. For his composition the painter has taken a low, close viewpoint so that the spectator has the impression of being surrounded by the panelling of the theatre and is thus as it were invited to step into the scene and take part in the lesson (fig. 18). By depicting the corpse extremely foreshortened and lit from directly above, Rembrandt achieved an extraordinarily powerful effect of contrast in which the dissecting table seems almost to project from the surface of the painting. Looking between the dead man's feet we see straight into the opened chest cavity. The low viewpoint forces us to look up to Dr Deijman, who is in the process of dissecting the brain.

One unusual detail in the *Anatomy Lesson of Dr Deijman* is that the head is still attached to the torso. In all other known illustrations of brain dissections the head has been separated from the rest of the body (see fig. 11), in accordance with the advice given by Vesalius in *De humani corporis fabrica libri septem* that the head and torso should be parted.[85] Rembrandt must have been familiar with one of the illustrations accompanying Vesalius's description, given the great similarities with his painting (fig. 19).[86] The print shows how, when the skin has been peeled back, the skullcap lifted and the membranous tissue removed, the two cerebral hemispheres are separate; in the painting, Deijman is in the act of using a lancet to lift the hard membrane (*'falx cerebri'*), marked with a 'D'. Given the suggested meanings of the anatomical action in Rembrandt's earlier anatomy lesson, it may be wondered whether the illustration of a brain dissection had some special significance to Deijman and the assembled surgeons. Vesalius treats the brain in the last book of the *septem libri*. To him, the human brain was the most exalted of all the parts of the body: it was the seat of the chief faculties and of the physical senses - '*cerebro principis animalisque facultatum sedi & sensuum organis*'.[87] It should also be pointed out that, for an anatomist, successfully completing the technically difficult dissection of the brain was a matter of some honour.

Rembrandt conveyed the time element in the anatomical action by using the opened abdomen to refer to the beginning of the lesson. There is a suggestion that the dissection has been resumed after a short break: the assistant holds not only the removed skullcap but also the sheet with which the *subjectum* had moments earlier been covered. Deijman has lifted the skull and separated the two cerebral hemispheres. Soon he will uncover the deeper parts of the brain. Dissection of the brain seems to be presented as the climax of the lesson: perhaps this is why the head is shown still attached to the body. Presumably carefully chosen details in the portrayal of the other now vanished sitters would originally have further enhanced the dynamic quality of the scene. In Rembrandt's drawing of the scene (fig. 17) we can see that the two surgeons sitting on the right are watching intently, while behind Deijman on the left someone is in the act of standing up to obtain a better view of what the prelector is doing.

Rembrandt's *Anatomy Lesson of Dr Deijman* may have been intended, in a way analogous to the *Anatomy Lesson of Dr Tulp*, as testimony to Deijman's learning, expressed in the *moment suprême* of his anatomical prowess. When interpreting what is left of the painting it is important to bear in mind that Deijman and Rembrandt were both faced with the task of surpassing the earlier painting. Perhaps this was why the picture was designed somewhat in the style of the title prints in anatomical treatises, which generally have the same kind of highly symmetrical structure (cf. fig. 13).[88] This might at least offer an explanation for what has been described as the traditional composition of Deijman's *Anatomy Lesson*.[89]

Dissecting Room in Meat Hall

From descriptions of the city we know that after the anatomy theatre was created in the Kleine Vleeshal in 1639 the Guild Chamber continued to be in the Anthoniswaag. It is important to make this perfectly clear because some authors have assumed that the Surgeons' Guild left the weigh-house in 1639 and did not return until 1691.[90] The city historian Melchior Fokkens referred to the splitting of dissecting room and Guild Chamber in 1662: 'Also in the Nes, above the hall in which St Peter's chapel used to be, there is a fine hall or dissecting room for the chirurgeons and physicians where the corpses of criminals who have been executed are cut open and examined so as to come to a thorough understanding of the human body; and the same surgeons have their chamber or meeting-place over the Weighing House on the New Market, whither all the surgeons of the city are obliged to come twice a week to attend lectures serving their practice. All who fail to attend are fined a certain fixed amount, and the lectures are given in Dutch, since we are best accustomed to our mother tongue.

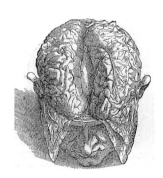

19. After Johann Stephan von Kalkar
Illustration of the Dissection of the Brain
Woodcut, 13 x 13 cm
Illustration from Andreas Vesalius, *De humani corporis fabrica libri decem*, Basle 1555, fol. 758
(Private collection U.S.A.)

In this chamber hang large and magnificent paintings, all pertaining to the chirurgeon's art.'[91]

In 1663, the year in which Olfert Dapper confirms these two locations,[92] the inventory of the Surgeons' Guild chamber was enriched with an unusual and special gift from a certain Jan Zeeuw, a *Cranium* by Hercules Segers (1589/90 – no later than 1638).[93] This painting may be identical with a small *Death's-head* which has in the past been attributed to Segers (fig. 20). This gift fitted in perfectly with the diverse collection of skeletons and specimens which constituted a suitable entourage for the five anatomy pieces hanging in the room.

In 1665 Isaac Commelin wrote: 'And that being in the guild chamber, now at the *Nieuwe Waagh* or former *St. Anthonis Poort* (described above, fol. 179): being a wonderfully spacious room, provided with chair, table and benches; decorated with some anatomical skeletons and paintings of past board members. Every Monday morning at eleven o'clock they have meetings to arrive at a settlement (after voluntary submission) of any disputes arising, whether passed on to them by the courts or otherwise occurring between patients and surgeons, masters and assistants.'[94]

A few pages before this the same writer gives a fairly detailed description of the dissecting room on the Nes, which is all the more interesting as there are no known illustrations of the interior: 'This [the dissection of human bodies] having commenced in this city, although the custom (it is said) is much older, uses the fact that this *cutting place* has been built after the fashion of the Roman theatres, high and round, having in the middle a long turning table for dissecting the dead body, surrounded on all sides by five or six rising circles so that it can be seen by a large crowd of spectators. The dissector (who is a master of Medicine) stands before it in order, turning round, to lecture to the audience. Hanging directly above it to light it is a large and handsome brass chandelier. The room is further embellished with all sorts of skeletons both human and animal, as well as a fully equipped case of dissecting instruments.'[95]

If Rembrandt's *Anatomy Lesson of Dr Deijman* had not been largely destroyed by fire, this last quotation would doubtless have provided the basis for a debate concerning the degree to which the painting accorded with reality. In any event, the descriptions of the guild chamber and dissecting theatre give us a lively picture of the surgeons' activities and the surroundings in which they took place. We know that the collection of paintings remained in the Guild Chamber, which was also decorated with a number of skeletons. The description of the layout of the anatomy theatre evokes associations with the *Theatrum Anatomicum* in Leiden (fig. 4).

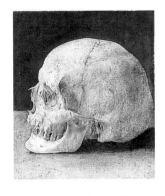

20. Hercules Segers (?)
Death's-head
Canvas, 29.2 x 26 cm
Private collection

21. Adriaen Backer
The Anatomy Lesson of Dr Frederik Ruysch, 1670
Canvas, 168 x 244 cm
Amsterdams Historisch Museum, inv. no. A 2000

Frederik Ruysch: Anatomy as Art

Frederik Ruysch (1638-1731) was originally an apothecary in The Hague before becoming a *doctor medicinae* at the university of Leiden in 1664. He continued to live in The Hague until his appointment as *praelector anatomiae* in 1666, the year in which Jan Deijman died. Unlike his predecessor, Ruysch went on to become a versatile medical scientist who enjoyed an international reputation and was the author of many publications.[96] It was while still a student at Leiden that he had applied himself to the preservation of corpses and the preparation of individual parts of the body.[97] His techniques for injecting hot, rapidly setting liquids made it possible to prepare anatomical subjects in advance, the added pigments making for a lifelike appearance. The method meant that it was now possible in principle to demonstrate dissection all the year round, irrespective of the ambient temperature.[98] Ruysch gave his first public anatomy lesson in 1667; of the total of 31 lessons recorded, six took place outside the winter months.[99]

In the early spring of 1670 the corpse of a certain Pasquier Joris from Ypres served as a *subjectum*; the man had been executed by hanging on 29 March. On the five succeeding days Ruysch demonstrated anatomy 'above the hall, in the usual place.'[100] For this particular lesson, then, we can more or less rule out the possibility that the prelector prepared the cadaver in advance of his performance. Nor does it seem likely that he used the event primarily to demonstrate his embalming and injection techniques. However, he does seem to have seized the occasion to have himself painted, together with a group of surgeons, by Adriaen Backer (1635/36-1684), whose *Anatomy Lesson of Dr Frederik Ruysch* is dated 1670 (fig. 21).[101] Comparing the names of the sitters with those shown in the guild's *Anatomieboek* as having attended the lesson again produces some discrepancies, though this need not come as a surprise: two of the wardens present had already had their portraits painted in 1656.[102]

The composition unmistakably betrays the influence of the *Anatomy Lesson of Dr Tulp* (fig. 12), except that this time the surgeons are ranged along both sides of the dissecting table. In addition the subject, highly foreshortened, is reminiscent of that in the *Anatomy Lesson of Dr Deijman* (fig. 16). In the light of the fragmentary state of the Rembrandt work, the extent to which Backer consulted Rembrandt's second *Anatomy Lesson* for the background remains uncertain. However, Backer too created suitable surroundings for a dissection, albeit not by suggesting the tiers of seating in an anatomical theatre, as Rembrandt had (see figs 17 and 18). The classical architecture of the theatre, adorned with pilasters and busts in niches, endows the dissection in the foreground with an international allure quite in keeping with the ambitions of the young prelector Ruysch. It may be that Backer, like Rembrandt before him, drew on the iconography of the frontispieces of anatomical literature (cf. fig. 13).[103] The classical sculptures are usually identified as Apollo and Asclepius, the gods of medicine.[104]. On the pilaster to the right there is a list of names and numbers to assist in identifying the sitters. Both the curtailed niches and the incomplete list of names point to the painting having been trimmed at the top.[105]

One of the interesting features of this painting is the outwardly directed gaze and pointing gesture of the surgeon on the extreme right. It is certain that the painting was not trimmed on the right, since the edge very clearly shows the original cusping of the canvas. This means that the surgeon's pose and gesture must be interpreted as an invitation to the spectator to share in the lecture being given by Ruysch, to whom he is pointing. The gesture, which is quite in accordance with the tradition of the undamaged anatomy pieces of 1619 and 1632 (figs 7 and 12), may have had something to do with the intended placing of the painting in the guild chamber: it is easy to imagine how a visitor entering the room would become aware of the scene from right to left. This might also explain the light entering from the right of the picture.

More curious than the composition, however, is the way the corpse has been painted. Indeed, there is very little to show that it is a corpse at all, in contrast to the two previous anatomy pieces by Rembrandt. It is difficult to see how the practically undamaged state of the body cannot have some specific significance transcending the general tendency towards a more elegant style of painting in the 1660s.[106] Hansen has recently demonstrated convincingly that the rendering of Backer's subject for dissection is deliberately flattering in order to lend emphasis to the prepared state of the corpse - perhaps on Ruysch's own instructions. Painting the body in this way is a reflection of Ruysch's stature as an anatomist and, in particular, of his skill in embalming and preparing cadavers.[107] It was thanks to his revolutionary methods that the spectators at anatomy lessons no longer had to endure the *subjectum* as a body undergoing the inevitable process of putrefaction.[108] The anatomical procedure shown in the painting - showing the lymph glands in the groin once the skin of abdomen and left thigh had been peeled back - is a reference to Ruysch's research and what was at that time his only publication,[109] but it is subordinate to the idealized representation of the youth on the dissecting table. The raised right leg, somewhat obscuring our view of the section, is incompatible with a lifeless body and suggests a state of slumber rather than death. This means that it is unlikely to be the actual body of the executed Pasquier Joris.[110]

Two years before the painting of Backer's anatomy piece, the authorities had appointed Frederik Ruysch to be the examiner for the city's midwives; in 1672 he was also charged with the teaching of midwifery.[111] Alongside his work as prelector he continued to refine his methods in the area of the preparation and preservation of corpses, assembling in his own house a large collection of preparations of both human and animal origin. As a botanist he also had a substantial natural history collection, and his 'cabinet', to which after 1673 he devoted a whole room, ultimately became famous all over the world and attracted large numbers of visitors. From later descriptions and his own publications on the subject of the collection we know that he produced a number of moralizing still-life pieces made entirely of organic material.[112]

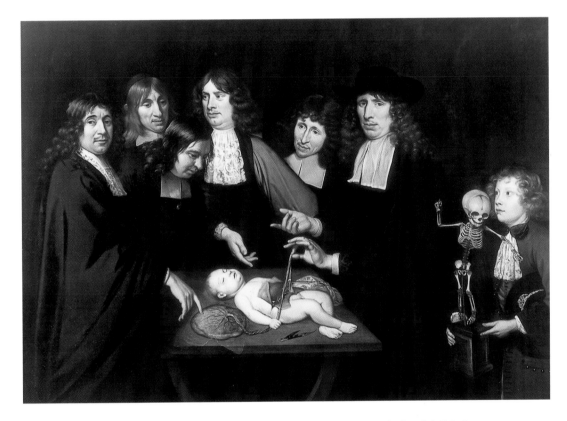

22. Jan van Neck
The Anatomy Lesson of Dr Frederik Ruysch, 1683
Canvas, 142 x 203 cm
Amsterdams Historisch Museum, inv. no. A 2644

In one of the most successful paintings by Jan van Neck (*c.* 1635-1714), dated 1683, five surgeons look on as Frederik Ruysch performs a dissection (fig. 22).[113] The most striking elements of this scene are the nature of the subject – not an executed criminal this time but a stillborn baby – and the presence of a young boy holding the skeleton of an infant. The skeleton could easily have been based on one of the examples in Ruysch's cabinet, and the boy has been identified as the prelector's son Hendrick, who was about ten years old at the time.[114] He is reported often to have assisted his father in preparing his subjects and subsequently followed in his footsteps, becoming a doctor himself. The presence of the boy is unique in an anatomy piece. In the picture the young Hendrick looks towards the surgeon on the extreme left, who in turn regards the spectator. Together they lead us into the scene. The four other surgeons are either engrossed in the demonstration or discussing it amongst themselves. Frederik Ruysch looks towards the spectator, so that the invitation to share in what is going on around the dissecting table ultimately comes back to the prelector himself.

Both the surgeons and the spectator outside the painting are shown explicitly how the placenta is connected to the infant by the umbilical cord. Van Neck took great pains to render the fine tissue of the placenta and umbilical cord as exactly as possible.[115] Against the background of the predominantly dark shades on the canvas, our attention is automatically drawn to the brightly lit body on the dissecting table, where the red of the open abdomen contrasts with the pale skin of the infant. Like the subject in the anatomy piece of 1670 (fig. 21), the child appears to be more asleep than dead. The peaceful calm that it radiates reminds one of Ruysch's famous preparations of infants' heads, a few of which still exist today.[116] The impression of sleep is subtly reinforced by the fact that the baby's hand grasps the umbilical cord.

Compared with the *Anatomy Lesson of Dr Tulp* and the metaphysical interpretations of which that painting is susceptible, much has changed: Van Neck's anatomy piece is more akin to a scientific record. We might almost be inclined to explain the child's disproportionate size in terms of the canvas's didactic function.[117] Ruysch seems keen above all to impress upon the spectator the importance of thorough training in obstetrical matters. At the same time his skill in preparing the bodily organs is again central to the picture. On the other hand there appears to be no particular moral tenor to this work: in comparison with the *memento mori* skeletons of Ruysch's later publication the one in the painting is reproduced as if, bubbling with *joie-de-vivre*, it were on the point of leaping from its stand.

Although Ruysch holds the record for the number of dissections performed in public by a prelector - the *Anatomieboek* lists 31 - no anatomy lesson is reported for 1683, the year in which Van Neck's group portrait was painted.[118] However, considering that for the first time since the painting of the anatomy piece of 1619 all the persons portrayed, with the exception of father and son Ruysch, held posts on the board of the guild,[119] it is worth pondering for a moment what reason

Ruysch and the surgeons might have had for having themselves painted in that particular year. This brings us to the first warden piece in the collection of the Surgeons' Guild.

In his list of the paintings owned by the guild Monnikhoff records a portrait of its six wardens, including the two examiners.[120] This portrait group (fig. 23), the first without an anatomy lesson, is usually ascribed to Nicolaes Maes (1634-1693).[121] On the basis of the list of names Monnikhoff gives, it seems likely that the canvas was executed between September 1679 and September 1680, the year in which the surgeons portrayed were wardens of the guild.[122] Because there is no lecturing prelector or anatomical demonstration, the group can direct all their attention to the spectator. The best known of the six is unquestionably Govert Bidloo (1649-1713), who was to receive the degree of *doctor medicinae* in 1682. He is the man seated in front of the table with one leg nonchalantly crossed over the other. Bidloo's name is linked principally to his *Anatomia humani corporis*, a work of anatomical plates illustrated by Gérard de Lairesse which came out in 1684, and it would not be surprising if the initiative for commissioning the painting came from this ambitious surgeon.[123] By now Ruysch had been prelector for thirteen years and had already had himself painted in that capacity, following the example set by most of his predecessors (see fig. 23). For the time being there was no suitable occasion for a new group portrait in prospect.

In the course of 1682 the board of the day protested against the hanging in the guild chamber of the warden group completed in 1680.[124] The new painting was hung in place of the *Osteology Lesson of Dr Sebastiaen Egbertsz* of 1619 (fig. 7), which had evidently been banished to 'another corner'.[125] Those objecting, all of whom had been wardens since September 1682, praised the earlier 'portraits of the professors of Surgery' and condemned an act which in their opinion testified to a lack of respect for 'the memory of such illustrious men'. From their list of the successors to Sebastiaen Egbertsz we can deduce that the paintings hanging in the Guild Chamber included the *Anatomy Lessons* of prelectors Fonteijn (see fig. 8), Tulp (fig. 12), Deijman (see fig 16) and Ruysch (fig. 21).

Conspicuous by its absence is Aert Pietersz's *Anatomy Lesson* of 1601-3 (fig. 1). This painting may have hung in the dissection theatre in the Kleine Vleeshal, where it must also have hung from between 1603 and 1619. The enormous canvas may have been moved back to its original location in 1639, when the anatomy theatre was opened, or in 1656, following the completion of Rembrandt's *Anatomy Lesson of Dr Deijman* (fig. 16). It has always been assumed that this last painting was first hung in the anatomy theatre on the Nes, an assumption based on the small squares at the top of the drawing of the framed painting (fig. 17), which were thought to be beams in the ceiling of the Kleine Vleeshal.[126] It is conceivable that on reflection the wardens of the guild decided to have Rembrandt's second anatomy piece hung in the weigh-house when an investigation showed that hanging such a tall picture would be hampered by the beams in the Kleine Vleeshal.

On 22 December 1682 burgomaster Witsen ruled in favour of the protesting board, as a result of which the *Osteology Lesson of Dr Sebastiaen Egbertsz* (fig. 7) was rehung in its old place. The record of the resolution in the surgeons' *Resolutieboek*, on 19 February 1683, was calculated to make it clear to all and sundry that the inappropriate action by Govert Bidloo and his associates was not to be repeated. It may be no coincidence that it was precisely those wardens who had registered their complaint who later in the same year had themselves painted by Van Neck in a second *Anatomy Lesson of Dr Frederik Ruysch* (fig. 22), with the exception of Pieter Muijser - who ironically enough appears in the group portrait of 1680 which had caused so much offence.[127] In other words, this whole disagreeable affair may have been what prompted the painting of the new anatomy piece. Frederik Ruysch's specialties, particularly in the field of obstetrics, provided sufficient points of contact for a suitable demonstration without there being a need for a public dissection.[128] Although the composition again shows similarities to the *Anatomy Lesson of Dr Tulp* (fig. 12), in several respects the painting could be interpreted as homage to the *Osteology Lesson of Dr Sebastiaen Egbertsz* and hence to the tradition as it was evidently perceived by the surgeons themselves.

From Prelectors to Wardens

The successful intervention of the surgeons in 1682 was unable to prevent the anatomy piece as a portrait type gradually disappearing in favour of portraits of small groups of wardens. So it was that three wardens had themselves painted in 1684 (fig. 24); their three colleagues on the guild's board had already gone before them in Van Neck's anatomy lesson (fig. 22).[129] Although the unknown painter carried out his commission in fairly amateurish fashion, it is important that in this second group portrait without a prelector a modest *subjectum anatomicum* was introduced in the form of a skull.

24. Unknown artist
Three Wardens of the Surgeons' Guild, 1684
Canvas, 71 x 112 cm
Amsterdams Historisch Museum, inv. no. A 3035

Similar references to the sitters' capacities in the surgical field were to become a regular feature of subsequent commissions.

The changing nature of the surgeons' portraits was doubtless determined partly by Frederik Ruysch's long term in office as prelector; he evidently felt there was no need for him to be portrayed giving an anatomy lesson for a third time.

Even the final removal of the dissection room in 1691 from the Kleine Vleeshal to the brand-new *Theatrum Anatomicum* in the Anthoniswaag (fig. 25), the fulfilment of a long-cherished wish of the Surgeons' Guild, failed to produce a new anatomy piece.[130] To provide the best possible lighting a substantial central dome was placed on the old weigh-house for the new anatomy theatre, which had been built at the city's expense.

The seating hierarchy was precisely defined: the first row was reserved for members of the city government, the inspectors of the *Collegium*

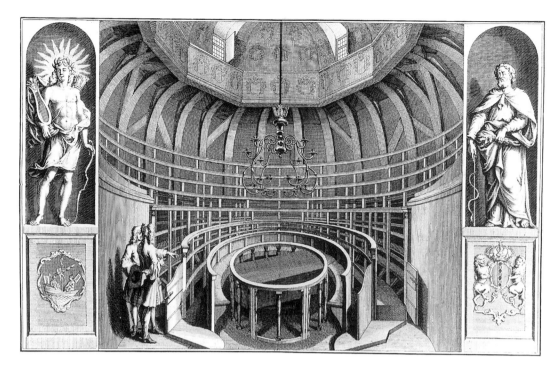

∨ 26. Jurriaan Pool
Two Surgeons with a Prepared Heart, 1699
Canvas, 74 x 115 cm
Leiden, Museum Boerhaave (on loan from Amsterdams Historisch Museum, inv. no. A 3031)

∨∨ 27. Unknown artist (Pieter Blauwpot?)
Three Wardens of the Surgeons' Guild, 1706
Canvas, 71 x 112 cm
Amsterdams Historisch Museum, inv. no. A 3012

∨∨∨ 28. Arnold Boonen
Five Wardens of the Surgeons' Guild,
1715-1716
Canvas, 160 x 250 cm
Amsterdams Historisch Museum, inv. no. A 2067

Medicum and doctors aged fifty and over, the second and third rows for other doctors, current and past members of the guild board, and for master surgeons aged fifty and over. Rows four, five and six were reserved for younger surgeons, and finally assistants and other visitors could take their seats in rows seven and eight. The dome was decorated with the arms of sitting wardens with, at the centre of it all, the arms of Frederik Ruysch.[131]

Whether the coats of arms presented an obstacle to commissioning new portraits is unclear. Eight years after the opening of the theatre two members of the guild had themselves painted with a prepared heart (fig. 26).[132] Like the stillborn baby in Van Neck's anatomy piece of 1683 (fig. 22), the heart was painted disproportionately large - a fact which has led some to suppose it to be the heart of a cow.[133] The painter, Jurriaan Pool (1666-1745), was Frederik Ruysch's son-in-law: in 1695 he had married Ruysch's daughter, the famous flower-painter Rachel Ruysch. The striking *subjectum* in the double portrait is undoubtedly a reference to Ruysch's preparation techniques.[134] With their inviting expression and the pride with which the surgeons hold up their work of art and the instruments they used to make it, it looks as if they are addressing themselves primarily towards the prelector himself, as if he were their most important spectator. For Jurriaan Pool, incidentally, after this commission there was to be only a relatively modest role in the surgeons' scheme of things: in 1700 he cleaned a number of paintings in the guild's collection (see p. 39).

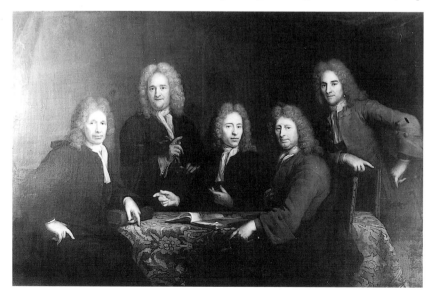

Pool's charming double portrait is the climax of an uneven little group of paintings all of about the same format. The commissions of 1684 and 1699 were followed in 1706 by a painting commissioned by three wardens who again had themselves painted with a skull (fig. 27).[135] The not particularly edifying result begs the question of whether this is not perhaps a rare work by the unknown painter Pieter Blauwpot (1655-after 1709), who three years later was to clean twelve of the guild's paintings (see p. 40). Things change for the better in 1716, the year in which Arnold Boonen (1669-1729) completed a warden piece (fig. 28) comparable in flair to Maes's painting of 1680 (fig. 23).[136] This time the attributes consist of a trepanning drill, used for drilling holes in skulls and bone, and a book by the French doctor Ambroise Paré (1517-1590), known principally for his revolutionary method of tying off blood vessels during operations instead of cauterizing them.[137] Boonen's convincing warden piece may be regarded as the start of a final flourishing of the surgeon group portrait in Amsterdam.

In any account of the paintings owned by the Surgeons' Guild in Amsterdam, the small but distructive fire of 8 November 1723 is bound to occupy a central place. From the scarce details that we have of it, it seems that the fire started on the first-floor landing, which was separated from the guild chamber by a wooden wall.[138] Pickenoy's *Anatomy Lesson of Dr Fonteijn* and Rembrandt's *Anatomy Lesson of Dr Deijman* probably hung on the other side of this partition and were exposed to the full force of the fire. The calamitous result is well known (figs 8 and 16).[139] Seen in the context of the collection as a whole it says a lot that the two canvases were not thrown out but patched up and made as presentable as could be expected.[140] It also looks very much as though the commission for the last anatomy piece *pur sang*, which went to Cornelis Troost in 1728, was occasioned by the mutilation of the two earlier pieces and the consequent availability of hanging space.

Cornelis Troost (1696-1750) was a pupil of Arnold Boonen who had established his reputation in 1724 with a portrait of the inspectors of the *Collegium Medicum*.[141] Four years later it fell to this young painter - whose position at the time was not entirely dissimilar to that of Rembrandt in 1632 - to prove himself again with a group portrait for the Surgeons' Guild. In this anatomy piece the chief role is played not by the now distinctly elderly Frederik Ruysch but by his assistant and later successor Willem Röell (1700-1775) (fig. 29). In practice Röell had already taken over from Ruysch when it came to teaching dissection, so the painting can be interpreted as a visual reminder of his appointment in 1727. That appointment, was not wholly without its detractors, and the wardens of the guild would later complain at intervals about their prelector's devotion to duty.[142] Incidentally, Röell does not seem to have given a public anatomy lesson in 1728; according to the *Anatomieboek* his first public performance did not take place until 25 January 1729.[143] Accordingly we can only guess at the former identity of the wonderfully realistically rendered corpse.

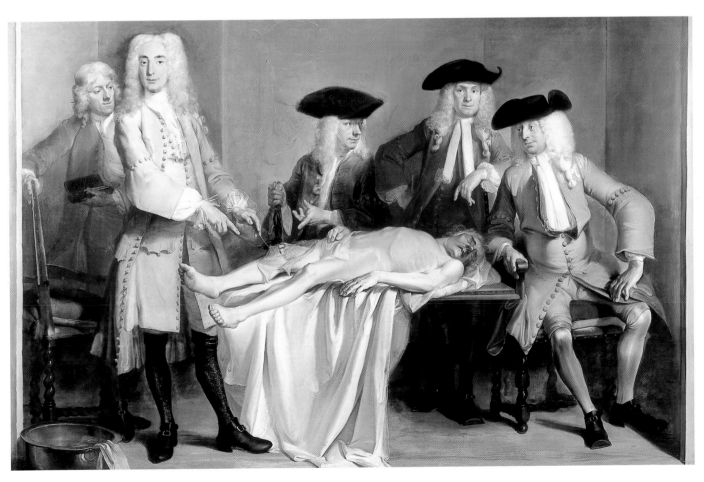

The choice of an anatomy piece instead of a warden portrait like the preceding four pieces in the collection may have been occasioned, as observed above, by the sensitive loss of two of the largest anatomy pieces in the collection. The dimensions of Troost's painting must have been quite close to those of Rembrandt's *Anatomy Lesson of Dr Deijman* before it was damaged (see fig. 18).[144] Both Röell and Troost took every opportunity to follow in the footsteps of their illustrious predecessors. Things had never been so quiet in an anatomy piece. The three wardens missing from the painting, who had been appointed in 1727-8, had no reason to have themselves painted as they already appeared in Boonen's warden piece of 1716 (fig. 28).[145] On the other hand the group has been joined by the guild assistant,[146] who watches prelector Röell from behind as he demonstrates the working of the knee joint to two wardens and an examiner.

Like Ruysch in 1683, Röell looks meaningfully at the spectator, drawing him into the scene. With the unusual full-length portrayal and the disposition of those present facing the spectator, Troost has created an exceedingly realistic and theatrical effect which doubtless contributed to the great appreciation with which this piece has been viewed ever since it was painted.[147]

A preliminary drawing for the painting shows a far more ambitious composition (fig. 30): the guild assistant was originally to have stood on the steps of an anatomy theatre, forming a link between the group in the foreground and a raised rear plane with three surgeons looking on. Although the canvas appears at some time to have been trimmed and the height of the guild chamber does not rule out the painting once having been as tall as the drawing suggests, it seems more probable that Troost was forced to abandon his grandiose plans when it became clear that only three of the six wardens were to sit for the picture.[148] However, he was to exact his artistic revenge only a year later in another colossal group portrait: the *Regents of the Almoners' Orphanage*.[149]

In 1731 Troost was able to confirm his reputation with the Surgeons' Guild with a highly convincing portrait of three wardens who had not previously been painted (fig. 31).[150] For identification purposes their arms were painted on the background: a novelty for the guild, possibly inspired by the coats of arms in the dome over the *Theatrum Anatomicum*. There are no medical

attributes, but the writing pose of the man in the middle and the certificate held by the warden on the left are references to these surgeons' tasks as governors. Yet it was precisely activities of this kind that were to provide the basis for an incident unparalleled in the history of the Surgeons' Guild. At the instigation of warden Abraham Titsingh, who joined the board on 6 September 1731, the city authorities instituted an investigation into alleged fraudulent activities on the part of board members. The results showed that ever since 1728 there had been dishonest dealings relating to surgeons' diplomas – and embezzlement of the guild's funds on a large scale.[151] Following on from these revelations, on 24 January 1732 all the wardens of the guild were removed from office 'for their wrong management'. Even former wardens did not escape. With only one exception they had all been painted in their capacity as warden or examiner by Boonen or Troost,[152] and in satirical poems of 1732 fun was made of their portraits in the Guild Chamber.[153]

It is not beyond the bounds of probability that it was on account of the tumultuous events within the guild that Troost was passed over as the painter of the next warden piece. Be that as it may, the commission from the new board went not to him but to Jan Maurits Quinkhard (1688-1772), another former pupil of Boonen's (fig. 32). Significantly, on 7 April 1732 the guild's minute-book records that the wardens were to have their portraits painted 'each at his own expense without charge to the guild, and to donate the painting to the guild, a painting in which the said wardens shall be portrayed, in commemoration of their appointment for the reformation of this guild, by the honourable Mr Quinkhard, painter'.[154] This is unquestionably a veiled sideswipe at the fraudulent wardens who had evidently even gone so far as to pay for their portraits out of the guild's coffers.

Like Troost the previous year, Quinkhard placed the emphasis on the administrative capacities of the surgeons he was portraying, though now the message to the spectator is different. Surrounded by the attributes of a governing board, the new members bear witness to their incorruptibility - led, naturally, by Abraham Titsingh on the extreme right.[155] In the background hangs a portrait of prelector Willem Röell, whose likeness appears to have been borrowed from Troost's anatomy piece (fig. 29). The completed group portrait was handed over to the guild on 15 September 1732, not long after the annual change of board. From the account of the handing-over we may deduce that the painting cost around six hundred guilders, not counting the portrait of the prelector.[156]

In the minute-book there is a telling note by Titsingh to the effect that 'they find it necessary to record that in order to hang their painting they have not placed any other piece at a disadvantage, and that all the damage done to the old and even the newer pieces, most recently to that of the painter Boonen, was done before they themselves ever thought of becoming wardens. Accordingly they wish, by recording this, to invite those who follow to think well of them and of their painting, by which no one has been injured and which serves solely as a memorial and likeness of the six wardens who reformed the guild.' Unfortunately there is no mention of which other paintings are meant by the reference to 'damage', but in any event five days later the *Anatomy Lessons* of Dr Fonteijn and Dr Tulp were handed over after restoration by Quinkhard.[157]

Quinkhard was to execute two more group portraits for the surgeons (figs 33 and 34). The space that the three substantial canvases must have taken up in the Guild Chamber suggests that at least some of the other paintings must have been moved to make way for them. From the record of the handing-over of the first warden piece in 1732, however, it seems that the board left the paintings

32. Jan Maurits Quinkhard
The Wardens of the Surgeons' Guild, 1732
Canvas, 176.5 x 273 cm
Amsterdams Historisch Museum, inv. no. A 454

33. Jan Maurits
Quinkhard
*Seven Members of the
Surgeons' Guild*, 1738
Canvas, 193 x 275 cm
Amsterdams Historisch
Museum, inv. no. A 454

34. Jan Maurits
Quinkhard
*Four Wardens of the
Surgeons' Guild*, 1744
Canvas, 162 x 236 cm
Amsterdams Historisch
Museum, inv. no. A 7390

already in the chamber undisturbed. In his painters' biographies of 1750-1 Jan van Gool describes both the two paintings by Troost and the three by Quinkhard, but Jan Wagenaar, in his history of Amsterdam of 1765, refers only to the pieces by Boonen and Quinkhard, in addition to the group portrait by Tibout Regters, to be described below (see fig. 35).[158] In the light of the dented reputations of the wardens in the two Troosts, it would be no great surprise if precisely these two works had been removed at some point. The framed portrait of Röell seen in Quinkhard's first warden piece (fig. 32) perpetuated the prelector's presence in the Guild Chamber. His incorruptibility is emphasized by the caption 'VIGILATE JUSTE' beside his head. Quinkhard's next two group portraits (figs 33 and 34) make no political statement; indeed, here the attributes of surgery have returned to the boardroom table.

The great helmsman of the reform of 1732, Abraham Titsingh, was the only surgeon to have himself painted twice. He would undoubtedly have been aware that until then only the prelectors Sebastiaen Egbertsz and Frederik Ruysch, both doctors of medicine, were represented by two portraits in the guild chamber. In Quinkhard's warden piece of 1738 he is seen standing behind the middle of the table (fig. 33). Apart from secretarial requisites the table carries a display of bladder stones and the instruments for removing them. The man with the surgical instruments has been identified as Hermannus Meijer, who conducted many operations for the removal of stones.[159] Of the surgeons depicted, whose identities are confirmed by the coats of arms, only four, later five, were on the board in the guild year 1737/38.[160] In other words, for the first time since 1670 we have a group portrait of the Surgeons' Guild which includes ordinary members of the guild, a practice that had hitherto been confined to the anatomy pieces. The old title of this painting, *Seven Wardens of the Surgeons' Guild*, would in any case have been recognized as inaccurate for the simple reason that under the guild's statutes it was impossible for seven wardens to serve at the same time.

Among the four wardens who had themselves painted by Quinkhard in 1744 their administrative qualities have clearly been subordinated to their aspirations in the field of surgery (fig. 34).[161] Apart from the ink-stand on the table, the skull, a humerus and a large illustration of a human skeleton testify above all to anatomical skills. The illustration, after a drawing by Jan Wandelaar (1690-1759), comes from *De ossibus corporis humani* by the Leiden anatomist Bernhard Albinus (1697-1770), which was published in 1726.[162] One of the surgeons is holding the book itself, with the inscription 'ALBIN - De ossibus' on the spine. Considering the emphasis on human anatomy in the picture and the presence of *subjecta anatomica* on the table, one might almost be inclined to regard the prelector as conspicuous by his absence. It is unclear whether the choice of attributes which seem to bestow some prelectoral dignity on the wardens was in any way influenced by the deteriorating relations between Willem Röell and the surgeons at this time.[163] That the skull on the table is strikingly similar to the one in the *Anatomy Lesson of Dr Johan Fonteijn* (fig. 8) need occasion no surprise: that old anatomy piece had, after all, been restored by Quinkhard in 1732.[164] Both his paintings of skulls were probably based on the same example, possibly a drawing, the skull of 1744 being a mirror image of the substitute *subjectum* in Pickenoy's anatomy piece.

In the light of the dissecting pretensions of the wardens portrayed in it, Quinkhard's third commission for the guild might have been a worthy conclusion to the series of group portraits of the surgeons were it not for the fact that in 1758 Tibout Regters (1710-1768) painted the last genuine anatomy piece, complete with surgeons, *subjectum* and prelector (fig. 35). Regters was a pupil of Quinkhard's and had some years previously won his spurs with a group portrait for the *Collegium Medicum*, as Troost had before him.[165] In contrast to Troost's *Anatomy Lesson of Dr Röell* (fig. 29), however, the action takes something of a subordinate role. Prelector Petrus Camper (1722-1789) stands to the right of the table, demonstrating the lie of muscles and nerves in the neck by reference to a severed head placed upside-down in a holder. Camper had taken up his duties as prelector in 1755, the year of his appointment as professor at the Athenaeum Illustre (the precursor of the modern University of Amsterdam).[166] Although Röell was formally still in his post, it was Camper who provided the surgeons with instruction in the skills of dissection. The commissioning of Tibout Regters for an anatomy piece was perhaps the consequence of the good relations between the new prelector and the surgeons.[167]

Whereas in Quinkhard's painting of 1744 the skull and bones figure in a surgical tête-à-tête amongst the wardens, in Regters's work the *subjectum* and the prelector are both guests at a meeting of the guild board: even the oriental table-cloth has not been removed. Regters must have struggled with his commission: on the one hand he had to present an anatomy lesson, on the other the picture looks most of all as if it is trying to be a group portrait of six wardens, with the guild's assistant on the

35. Tibout Regters
The Anatomy Lesson of Prof. Petrus Camper, 1758
Canvas, 169 x 329 cm
Amsterdams Historisch Museum, inv. no. A 7391

extreme left.[168] Apart from some polite sideways glances the wardens appear to be having difficulty in evincing any interest in what Camper is doing. To put it another way, the surgeons are interested chiefly in their own portraits whereas the prelector seems to be addressing himself mainly to the spectator, as Röell and Ruysch had done before him. On the baroque tripod in front of the table there is a brass bowl with a sponge, a reference to the old combination of barber-chirurgeon which also appears in the very first anatomy piece for the guild (fig. 1). Regters could not have surmised that his painting would be the last anatomy piece of them all. Without realizing it, he had created the synthesis - albeit somewhat laboured - of the warden portrait and the anatomy piece.[169]

Conclusion

None of the anatomy pieces of the Amsterdam Surgeons' Guild is an exact representation of a particular event; rather, they are all group portraits, executed to commemorate the tenure of a *praelector anatomiae* or membership of the Surgeons' Guild. In anatomical terms, indeed, they are far removed from reality: only in the *Anatomy Lesson of Dr Jan Deijman* (fig. 16) is there any reference to the correct order in which dissections were performed. Moreover each of these pictures shows only a limited number of surgeons, a fact which reflects the custom by which each had to pay for his own portrait. And of the many spectators who were wont to attend public anatomy lessons there is no trace whatever.

The anatomy lesson was both a suitable occasion and a fitting subject for a group portrait. This certainly seems to apply to the early *Anatomy Lesson of Dr Sebastiaen Egbertsz* (fig. 1), in which all the surgeons in the guild at the time were portrayed, and perhaps equally to the *Anatomy Lesson of Dr Willem Röell* (fig. 29). The *Anatomy Lesson of Dr Nicolaes Tulp* (fig. 12), Backer's *Anatomy Lesson of Dr Frederik Ruysch* (fig. 21) and the *Anatomy Lesson of Dr Jan Deijman* (fig. 16) have in common that they can be linked to a documented event. Yet only in the case of the last of these do we know for certain that the commission was given to mark the first official act by a prelector as an anatomist to the guild. The *Osteology Lesson of Sebastiaen Egbertsz* (fig. 7) and the *Anatomy Lesson of Johan Fonteijn* (fig. 8) may have been occasioned by the moving of the Guild Chamber to the old weigh-house and its furnishing respectively. Only the commissioning of the *Wardens of the Surgeons' Guild* of 1732 (fig. 32) can be convincingly shown to have been prompted by political motives.

From the dispute in 1682 concerning the hanging of Maes's warden piece (fig. 23) it is clear that in surgical circles the older paintings were regarded as a group that could not be broken up, which told and symbolized the history of the guild. Confirmation of respect for the guild's own traditions is provided by what happened after the fire of 1723, when it was decided that the damaged canvases should be kept and repaired. The hanging of Quinkhard's warden portrait in 1732 also went hand-in-hand with great respect for the earlier paintings.

From the painting of the first warden piece in 1680, the surgeons attached as much importance to a portrait in such a work as to one in an anatomy piece, and for that reason alone the warden pieces should not be seen as separate from the far more spectacular *Anatomy Lessons*. If they were, the anatomy pieces might invite rash speculation as to their meaning and be saddled with far-fetched interpretations.[170]

In the context of this survey we may conclude that the length of Frederik Ruysch's prelectorate signalled the end of the tradition of anatomy pieces in the Amsterdam Surgeons' Guild, in spite of his leading role in two of them.[171] With the *Anatomy Lesson of Dr Willem Röell* (fig. 29) as a late exception, in the group portraits painted from 1684 onwards the dissecting table was gradually replaced by the boardroom table, on which only the added attributes inform us that the persons round the table are surgeons.

Thanks to the archival material that has survived we know almost all the names of the people portrayed, as indeed we know the names of the wardens on the ever-changing board. Combining these two sets of names produces some interesting observations about the perceived need for portraits within one and the same guild. The overview that is created in this way is all the more fascinating because most of the painters selected for these commissions were far from obscure. As a result, the anatomy pieces and warden pieces of the Amsterdam Surgeons' Guild together make up a series of paintings that is unrivalled in the history of Dutch art.

II Under the Scalpel Twenty-one Times
The Restoration History of the *Anatomy Lesson of Dr Nicolaes Tulp*

Ben Broos and Jørgen Wadum

The Rembrandt Research Project's most recent judgement of the *Anatomy Lesson of Dr Nicolaes Tulp* is that it is a 'moderately well preserved, authentic and relatively well documented work, reliably signed and dated 1632.'[1] Strictly speaking, the epithets 'moderately', 'relatively' and 'reliably' are mere palliatives. In fact, following severe neglect the painting must have been repeatedly 'fixed up' in the course of time. The most recent restoration in part prompted the idea of writing a survey of all of the restorations the painting endured throughout the centuries.

As early as 1918, Willem Martin (1876-1954), director of the Mauritshuis from 1909 to 1945, had pointed out the usefulness of writing such an account of restorations: 'The cleaning of paintings previously frequently treated is an extremely thankless task, because the last "restorer", naturally, is held responsible for overcleaning the painting. Therefore, it is important to clarify the history of the various restorations methods and related issues.'[2] Research into the past restoration of a painting, however, is complicated by all kinds of factors, first and foremost being the attitude of the previous restorers: generally speaking, the final result was always paramount, while describing the condition and the working method was not considered necessary. Moreover, given the competition or the experimental nature of the treatment applied one profited from keeping one's own method secret.[3]

The following is an attempt to reconstruct the history of the restoration of Rembrandt's *Anatomy Lesson of Dr Nicolaes Tulp* on the basis of a variety of extant documents. Between 1700 and 1952, the painting was restored at least 21 (!) times. Unfortunately, it proved impossible to gain a complete picture of the nature of these treatments from the sources concerning the painting.
The restoration history of this painting also yields an image of the development of the occupation of picture restorer in the Netherlands: from the seventeenth- and eighteenth century painter/craftsman-restorer, via the nineteenth-century connoisseur/picture restorer to the present-day museum restorer trained in a conservation-restoration discipline based on the natural sciences.

The Painter-Restorers (1700-1840)

Despite the historical significance of Rembrandt's *Anatomy Lesson of Dr Tulp*, this work was first described in documents at a surprisingly late date. No archival document has surfaced relating to the commission of this group portrait, and in 1662 the Amsterdam city chronicler Melchior Fokkens referred only generally to the 'large excellent paintings all concerning the art of the healers' in the building of the Old Meat Market on the Nes.[4] One of the next references is a passage in Caspar Commelin's *Vervolg van de beschryving der stadt Amsterdam* of 1693, in which he explicitly praises the masterpieces by Rembrandt in the anatomical theatre in the Waag, or Weighhouse, namely the group portrait with Dr Tulp and the *Anatomy Lesson of Dr Deyman* (Amsterdam, Rijksmuseum):[5] 'This room is not only decorated with some human and animal skeletons, but also with various paintings done by unusually artful painters, including two by the celebrated Rembrant which surpass; they illustrate the same subject of a man being dissected by the then *Professor Anatomiae* surrounded by the masters in the service of the guild.'[6]

Between 1639 en 1691 the Theatrum Anatomicum was located in the Nes, but the Surgeons' Guild kept its quarters at the Anthoniswaag. The above-mentioned paintings by Rembrandt hung there in the guild chamber on the first floor (see p. 13, fig. 6).[7]

On 29 January 1700, according to the guild's *Grootboeck*, the Amsterdam surgeons paid 25 guilders for the 'cleaning of all the paintings in the college.'[8] This was done by the painter Jurriaan Pool (1665-1745), the son-in-law of Professor Frederik Ruysch who succeeded Dr Deijman as prelector, or reader, of the guild in 1666. Pool, thus, was the first restorer of the *Anatomy Lesson of Dr Tulp*.

Because the painting was only 68 years old in 1700, the cleaning may only have consisted of the removal of surface dirt. It may also possibly have been rubbed with new varnish to restore its shine.[9] Although the varnish does not appear to have been removed, this would have been possible at the time. In an advertisement in the *Amsterdamse Courant* of 1690, a certain 'konstschilder', or art painter, Markus Kortsz., writes that he had found a 'powerful substance that thins all varnishes on paintings to such an extent that it can be removed with a sponge.'[10]
The composition of this wonder product has not come down to us.

In the summer of 1709, the painter Pieter Blauwpot (1655–after 1709) was commissioned by the guild to clean 12 paintings, for which, according to the receipt, he received 14 guilders.[11]

> We know that Blauwpot regularly provided paintings with new varnish, possibly to enhance the transparency of the varnish that had become dull or cracked due to moisture.

Two years later, the German globetrotter Zacharias Conrad von Uffenbach visited the Waag. Apparently, the boy who showed him the paintings waxed enthusiastic about the *Anatomy Lesson of Dr Deyman*, but Von Uffenbach was primarily moved by a canvas hanging to the right of the mantlepiece, which he deemed 'incomparable'. 'In this work, the famous anatomist Tulp is performing the dissection. For this [painting] a still living burgomaster here offered a thousand Thaler, which is then certainly quite handsome.'[12] The renowned aspiring buyer could have been Burgomaster Nicolaes Witsen (1641–1717).

The eighteenth-century minutes of the Amsterdam Surgeons' Guild make repeated, explicit references to problems in connection with the condition of the *Anatomy Lesson of Dr Tulp*.[13] For instance, in 1723 a fire raged through a part of the guild chamber seriously damaging a number of anatomy pieces, including Rembrandt's *Anatomy Lesson of Dr Deyman*. It is not clear whether the anatomy piece with Dr Tulp also suffered from the heat in the room.

In May of 1732, though, the canvas was seriously affected by a 'a fiery smoke' emanating from a square hole in the chimney, which had long 'scorched' the paint surface. It was decided that 'all the paintings were to be made brighter or cleaned, and to repair the mantle of Professor N. Tulpius, [which had] flaked off.'[14]

> The 'brightening' of paintings was understood to mean the application of a varnish consisting of poppy-seed or turpentine oil locally to dull or dark spots. In this way, potential cracks and less than transparent areas were resaturated and the colours regained their depth.[15]

The skills of the painter Jan Maurits Quinkhard (1688-1772), who was to perform this task, were greatly respected. In April of 1732 he had also been awarded a commission to paint a group portrait of the surgeons (see p. 35, fig. 32).[16] On 20 September 1732, Quinkhard returned the restored canvas to the Waag. The minutes of the Surgeons' Guild report that 'the cloak of Sir professor Nicolaas Tulp, also burned and blistered, with paint even flaking off from the canvas in places, led the wardens of the guild to approve of providing the memorable and highly commendable professor with a new cloak.'[17] From this it appears that the 'restoration' of Tulp's coat was relatively drastic. It remains unclear just where other overpaintings were applied.

> With the help of a stereomicroscope and x-radiography one can see some wrinkles in the paint structure of the *Anatomy Lesson of Dr Nicolaes Tulp* that originated through intense heat. This can be observed chiefly in the upper section of the painting. In the *Anatomy Lesson of Dr Deyman*, large flaked off blisters could be observed as amorphous craters in the paint surface, which were the result of the fire that broke out nine years earlier, in 1723.[18]

The canvas was ravaged not only by smoke, but also by water. Quinkhard's assistance was invoked once again. The minutes of the guild of 16 October 1747 mention that: ' the guild servant Van der Waart informed the wardens of the guild that the painting of Tulp was damaged by leakage, whereupon the wardens told the guild servant to have it looked at by the carpenter and the painter J.M. Quinckhard.'[19]

> Traces of this minor disaster can be still be seen in the painting. In the right part is a vertical line of paint running straight through Dr Tulp, which has flaked off as a result of the water dripping on the painting. Water caused the canvas and a portion of the ground to swell and then shrink again once it had dried, whereby the paint cupped and eventually flaked off. This most likely also occurred along the bottom edge of the painting where it hung against a damp wall. A damp micro-climate arises immediately between the wall and the painting which can cause the same damage. Exposure to heat, possibly the fire of 1723, and certainly the 'fiery smoke' of 1732, reinforced this process.

In 1752, thus not even five years after Quinkhard's restoration, the painter Jan van Dijk (c. 1690-1769), in turn was asked to treat the painting: 'The wardens of the guild received permission from their most honourable sirs, the burgomasters, to mend and clean the painting of the honourable Professor Tulp by the painter Jan van Dijk, who has begun today [6 June 1752].'[20]

> Van Dijk (fig. 1) was entrusted with the management of the collection of paintings of the City of Amsterdam. He began his career as a painter in 1709 and as a restorer around 1746.[21] Unfortunately, we do not know how he worked, only that he 'cleaned, affixed, filled and varnished', which actually comprises the entire spectrum of conservation and restoration. Van Dijk described the works under his jurisdictions as 'maltreated vestiges of the art of painting.' In restoring them, he hoped 'to have discharged himself as an art-loving, prudent, and honest surgeon should, who heals the wounds of the maltreated persons, without leaving behind

mutilated parts, or even scars.'[22] Further, from Van Dijk's writings it is clear that he sharply criticised some of his fellow restorers as 'malicious people' who with their 'unskilled claws' attempted to preserve 'maltreated' paintings in the course of time.[23] Van Dijk's attitude can partly be explained by a growing historical awareness. Less and less did people try to restore a painting in keeping with the taste and views of their own time, considering it rather as a historical document to be returned to its original condition.[24]

Despite the permanent bad condition of the paintings, in 1765 the city chronicler Jan Wagenaar was nonetheless proud of the works in the Waag: 'the two oldest and most beautiful are both by Rembrandt: the loveliest of the two was painted in the year 1632, and shows Doctor Tulp and the surgeons Jacob Blok, Hartman Hartmansz., Adriaan Slabbraen, Jacob de Witt, Matthys Kalkoen, Jacob Koolveld and Frans van Loenen, all of whom except the latter were also wardens.'[25]

This enumeration makes the impression that Wagenaar had copied the names of the surgeons from the paper held by Hartman Hartmansz. The numbers before these names correspond with the numbers near each portrait head. These inscriptions were not made by Rembrandt, but added later (see p. 55-56). It is conceivable that Jurriaan Pool, Pieter Blauwpot or Jan Maurits Quinkhard at the time painted in the names and numbers at the request of the surgeons.[26]

1. Jan ten Compe, *Portrait of a Picture Restorer, robably Jan van Dijk*, Amsterdam Historical Museum, inv. no. SA 33842

In 1780 the College of Surgeons again requested a bid for the cleaning of the paintings in the guild chamber, this time from the Amsterdam artists Jan Ekels (1724-1781), Jacobus Buijs (1724-1801) and Julius H. Quinkhard (1734-1795). Buijs tendered the lowest offer and was awarded the commission, however upon further consideration he declined the honour as he was a professional painter and not a cleaning man. Quinkhard, on the other hand, was prepared to 'varnish, and fill the holes' in the painting, and even to 'touch it up.'[27]

The holes mentioned indicate that the condition of the original canvas was anything but optimal. Quite possibly, on this occasion Quinkhard was the first to provide the painting with a new lining canvas. Referring to the *Anatomy Lesson of Dr Tulp*, in 1817, the art-lover Goll van Franckenstein (1756-1821) wrote: 'That it [the painting] was spared solely due to the presence of the second canvas applied by Quinkhard.'[28]

The lining of paintings is one of the oldest techniques for preserving paintings on canvas, and was already in use in the seventeenth century.[29] In the late eighteenth and early nineteenth century, a paste lining was used. First, the paint layer was consolidated by attaching one or more layers of paper to the front of the painting. Subsequently the canvas was detached from the stretcher and restretched in a temporary frame. This frame, a *faux-chassis* or *les batteries*, was larger than the painting. Damp strips of paper were glued to the old canvas. Through the drying of the paper, which contracts, was achieved an initial stretching and planing (the flattening of deformations in the paint). A new canvas was stretched on a second stretcher, on which was brushed a paste consisting of a mixture of animal glue, syrup, balsam, and resin or a siccative oil. Following this the old canvas was laid on the new one and the two were joined by means of a hot iron or a press.[30] This treatment is very risky because the canvas can shrink quickly giving rise to cupping. Moreover, excessive pressure from the iron or press on the paint surface causes the canvas structure to become visible and flattens the paint. (fig. 2)

Quinkhard probably used this method. We do not know how he cleaned the painting, but the following recipe from 1767 affords two possibilities: 'To remove the varnish from some painting, take lavender oil and rub it gently over your paintings which will make it come off easily. Another. Take rectified spirits of wine and let it soak a little, then rub somewhat and clean.'[31] It should be clear that the work of the painter-restorer was still in an experimental and empirical phase.

2. The lining paste is being heated with a hot iron, photograph c. 1920

In 1781, one year after Quinkhard has refurbished the *Anatomy Lesson*, the English art critic Sir Joshua Reynolds (1723-1792) visited the surgeons' room in Amsterdam. The first painting that struck him was that of 'Professor Tulpius dissecting a corpse which lies on the table, by Rembrandt.' His commentary was largely factual. 'To avoid making it an object disagreeable to look at, the figure is but just cut at the wrist. There are seven other portraits coloured like nature itself, fresh and highly finished ... The dead body is perfectly well drawn, (a little fore-shortened) and seems to have been just washed. Nothing can be more truly the colour of dead flesh. The legs and feet, which are nearest the eye, are in shadow; the principal light, which is on the body, is by that means preserved in a compact form. All these figures are dressed in black.'[32]

When the guild was reorganised in 1796, the paintings in the Waag were appraised. 'A capital painting, representing a professor bent over a dead body and giving a Lesson, with seven other persons shown to the knees: by Rembrandt,' was valued by the agent Philippus van der Schleij at 3,000 guilders (fig. 3). The contrast with the remaining pieces was great: the group portraits by Backer, Troost and Quinkhard (see p. 27, 33, and 35, figs 21, 29 and 32) were only estimated at 60 to 100 guilders, and Rembrandt's *Anatomy Lesson of Dr Deyman* (it is true the worse for wear due to fire damage) at no more than 50 guilders.[33]

When the guilds were disbanded in 1798 under French rule, the art objects in the Waag became the responsibility of the Surgeons' Widows Fund, established especially for that purpose.

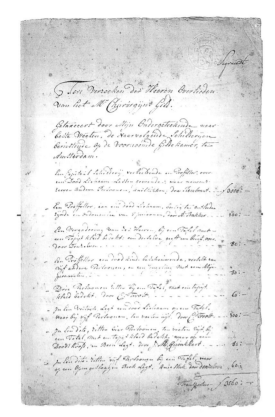

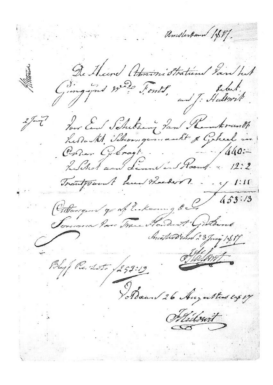

<< 3. The valuation report of Philippus van der Schleij, 1796

4. The bill of Hulswit, 1817

This institution had the paintings freshened up or restored several more times. In 1808, the art dealer-framemaker Jan Spaan (1744-1821) was involved 'as a cleaner of paintings to make the requisite reparations of the painting by Rembrandt in the guild chamber.'[34] The condition of its existence, however, remained wretched. The administrators of the fund were successively converting the treasures of the old guild into money. The time was ripe for outside intervention.

In a missive of 26 June 1817 to the commissioner for Education, Arts and Sciences, Cornelis Apostool (1762-1844), the director of the Rijksmuseum, complained about the indifferent way in which Rembrandt's masterpiece was dealt with. He was incensed about the fact that the work praised by the renowned connoisseur Reynolds hung in a room serving as a living room and kitchen to the guild servant and which was even heated in the summer. Furthermore, he pointed out that due to leaks 'almost the entire canvas had been damaged by rot' and that the paint threatened to fall off, but that the painting 'in an amazing way had been applied to another canvas, without having lost anything.'[35] As restorer, the fund's administrators had called upon the painter Jan Hulswit (1766-1822), who received payment of 440 guilders on 2 June 1817 after having 'relined, cleaned & entirely restored' Rembrandt's painting. For the 'advance for the canvas and stretcher' he received 12 guilders and 2 stuivers (fig. 4).[36]

> Hulswit, who was initially specialised in wallpaper painting, dedicated himself completely to restoring paintings as of 1807. His lining, the second one applied to the *Anatomy Lesson*, may well have been done in a fashion similar to the first. From his invoice it appears that he used rye-meal paste, poppy-seed oil and Venice turpentine for the glue mixture.[37] The varnish will have suffered greatly from the moisture of the glue paste and the heat of the iron and was therefore possibly removed. A new varnish was then applied after Hulswit had filled and retouched the lacunas with oil paint.[38]

Apostool naturally wanted to include the *Anatomy Lesson of Dr Tulp* in the collection of the Rijksmuseum then housed in the Trippenhuis. With his letter of 26 June 1817 he included a concept for a letter by the minister on behalf of the king to be sent to the Amsterdam local authorities as a way to achieve his goal. Minister Repelaer van Driel acted accordingly on 5 July 1817, without results however.[39]

Apostool arrived at his idea through a letter by Goll van Franckenstein to the Amsterdam local authorities dated 7 May 1817, in which the author expressed his concern for the condition of the *Anatomy Lesson*. He suggested that 'this artistic creation of Rembrandt's exalted genius be bought for a reasonable price ... by the City of Amsterdam and placed in its Town Hall.'[40] Goll's proposal, however, only led to a report by the treasurer of Amsterdam outlining financial and procedural problems, whereupon the matter was swept under the carpet.[41]

43

5. The poster for the auction of paintings on 4 August 1828

In AMSTERDAM, Anno 1828.

JERONIMO DE VRIES,
ALBERTUS BRONDGEEST,
ENG^T. MICH^L. ENGELBERTS,
EN
CORNELIS FRANÇOIS ROOS,
M A K E L A A R S.

Zullen op Maandag, den 4^den Augustus 1828, en volgende Dag, bij Voormiddags ten Tien Uren precies, ten Huize van de Wed. C. S. ROOS, in *Het Huis met de Hoofden*, op de Keizersgracht, tusschen de Leliengracht en Heerenstraat, door een baatloe geborgd BRAMBTE,

V E R K O O P E N:

EENE UITGEBREIDE EN VOORTREFFELYKE

VERZAMELING

VAN ZEER FRAAIJE

SCHILDERYEN

Waaronder veele door voorname Oude en Hedendaagsche Nederlandsche Meesters, en eenige mede van voorname Meesters uit de Fransche, Spaansche en Italiaansche Scholen.

Onder de Nederlandsche Meesters munten uit,

DIE VAN

L. BACKHUIZEN,	J. VAN DER HEYDE,	J. RUISDAAL,
N. BERCHEM,	J. KOBELL,	D. TENIERS,
O. VAN BERGEN,	F. VAN MIERIS,	J. VAN DER ULFT,
G. BERKHEYDEN,	A. VAN OSTADE,	W. VAN DE VELDE,
G. DOU,	C. POELENBURG,	A. VAN DER WERFF,
A. VAN DYK,	P. POTTER,	PH. WOUWERMAN;
G. VAN DER EEKHOUT,	P. P. RUBBENS,	

Als mede

HET WYD VERMAARDE EN ALOM BEROEMDE

MEESTERSTUK
VAN

REMBRAND,

Verbeeldende het Ontleedkundig Onderwys, door den Hoogleeraar **N. TULP,**

behorende aan het

CHIRURGYNS WEDUWEN-FONDS,

te Amsterdam.

Al hetwelke Verkocht zal worden ten Dage, Ure en Plaatse bovengemeld.

De Katalogusen zyn bij gemelde Makelaars, (à 25 Cents voor den Armen) te bekomen.

Alles twee Dagen voor de Verkoopdagen voor een ieder te zien.

Iemand nader onderrigting begerende, spreke met de Makelaars.

6. The receipt for collecting *the Anatomy Lesson of Dr Nicolaes Tulp,* 14 May 1828

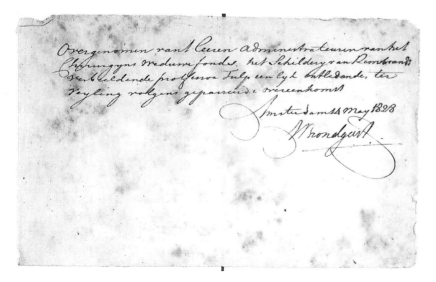

Even Apostool's appeal in his letter of 26 June 1817 for removing the painting from the Waag fell on deaf ears. By 1828 debates concerning Rembrandt's painting were raging at the highest level. On 28 April of that year, the administrators of the Surgeons' Widows Fund requested permission from the burgomasters and aldermen to sell the painting. They considered it a 'non-productive and unnecessary object for that fund.' Permission was promptly granted on 2 May.[42] The posters for the auction to be held on 4 August were printed up (fig. 5), and the catalogue could be obtained for 15 cents ('for the poor') from Cornelis François Roos in the *House with the Heads* in Amsterdam.[43]

On 13 May 1828, agent Roos informed the director of the Mauritshuis, Johan Steengracht van Oostkapelle (1782-1846), that a sale was coming up with superfluous paintings from the collection of the Rijksmuseum. 'At this sale' Roos wrote, as if nothing was going on, 'will be added the famous painting by Rembrand of the Anatomy Room, for which in my mind many foreigners will come over for, [and is] thus a fitting opportunity to sell something.'[44] A day later, Roos' colleague, Albertus Brondgeest, reported to the Waag in Amsterdam in order to collect the *Anatomy Lesson* 'for auction according to the agreement concluded,' as was recorded on the receipt (fig. 6).[45]

The Hague would appear to have been alarmed by the (never previously published) letter from Roos to Steengracht. On 19 May, the administrator of the Ministry of Education, Arts and Sciences, D.J. Van Ewijck, asked the governor of Noord Holland whether the upcoming sale of the masterpiece by Rembrandt was a fact and who its actual owner was.[46] On 7 June, the alarmed Van Ewijck informed the director of the Rijksmuseum that: 'It seems to me important to prevent the possibility of such a famous piece being sold to foreigners.'[47] Later that month, the Fourth Form of the Royal Dutch Institute protested the sale, with reference to the relining and restoration of 1817 which had been necessitated by the 'negligence of the owners, (which, had it not been found in time would have resulted in its total destruction).'[48] The insight and concern of several prominent individuals, as well as influential members of government, contrasts sharply with the avarice of the fund.

The *Amsterdamsche Courant* ran an advertisement on 19 July 1828 announcing the forthcoming sale.[49] However, in the meantime quiet diplomacy had had an effect, for on the same 19 July - upon advice of the minister, who had sought council from Apostool - the public sale of Rembrandt's *Anatomy Lesson of Dr Tulp* was forbidden by Royal Decree.[50]

7. F.L. Huijgens after Rembrandt, *the Anatomy Lesson of Dr Nicolaes Tulp*, engraving, 112 x 153 mm

1 Nicolaes Tulp
2 Jacob Block
3 Hartman Hartmansz
4 Adriaen Slabbraen
5 Jacob de Wit
6 Matthijs Calkoen
7 Jacob Colevelt
8 Frans van Loenen
and Aris Adriaensz, alias
Aris Kint

The *Amsterdamsche Courant* of 29 July ran an announcement that the sale 'by supreme order ... would not take place for the time being.'[51] A series of letters from and to the ministry, the Rijksmuseum, the Mauritshuis and the City of Amsterdam describe the further course of events.[52] Four appraisers were appointed. Representing the State were Cornelis Apostool and Johan Steengracht van Oostkapelle, and representing the fund the agents Jeronimo de Vries and Albertus Brondgeest. They set the value of the painting at 32,000 guilders. Amsterdam was unable to raise the money, and King Willem I subsequently wished that the painting be placed in the Mauritshuis in The Hague. 'His Majesty has been graciously pleased', Minister Van Ewijck wrote on 14 November 1828 to Steengracht, 'to charge that the painting by Rembrandt purchased from the Surgeons' Widows Fund in Amsterdam be placed in the Royal Cabinet [the Mauritshuis] here.'[53] Payment was made in two installments, in 1828 and 1829, as noted in the cash books of the fund.[54]

The intervention of the king symbolises, as it were, the recognition of Rembrandt's painting as an autonomous work of art rather than a relic of a no longer extant guild. For Apostool, the pill was bitter indeed since – as an insider – he knew that the purchase was actually financed by the proceeds of the paintings from the Rijksmuseum that were sold.[55] Steengracht van Oostkapelle, however, had the last laugh. In the fourth volume of his illustrated catalogue of the Mauritshuis (1830), the proud director concluded his selection of the hundred best paintings with an illustration of Rembrandt's group portrait (fig. 7). He informs us that 'It was decided that this work of art served as an appropriate ending to the publication of drawn images of the principal paintings in the Royal Cabinet.'[56] Since then, the *Anatomy Lesson of Dr Nicolaes Tulp* has continued to be one of the cornerstones of the Mauritshuis' fame.

The Painting Restorers (1841-1877)

Apostool and Steengracht van Oostkapelle must have been delighted with the rescue operation performed by the restorer Hulswit in 1817, yet in the course of time various parties in The Hague began to think otherwise. Shortly after taking up his appointment in May 1841, Steengracht's successor, Jean Zacharie Mazel (1792-1884), wrote a critical report on the Mauritshuis' collection which he sent to the minister along with a catalogue with notes regarding the condition of the paintings. About the *Anatomy Lesson of Dr Tulp*, he observed: 'The condition of the painting leaves much to be desired. When in 1815 or 1816 is was relined at the expense of the Surgeons' Guild in Amsterdam, the losses and damages were inadequately restored. Here and there the paint is flaking off and it is to be feared that this will worsen.'[57]

In the summer of 1841, Mazel had the painting restorer Nicolaas Hopman (1794-1870)[58] of Amsterdam overhaul the entire collection. On 31 July, Hopman submitted a declaration for the restoration of 291 paintings.[59] His handwriting is identical to that of the notes documenting his activities in a copy of the Mauritshuis catalogue of 1841.[60] For 'The anatomy lesson of Prof. Tulp' he had dispensed 7 guilders in material and work'.[61] While this was the highest price of all of the works he handled, in fact the treatment was relatively summary.

> Despite Mazel's disturbing remarks, Hopman deemed that the cleaning, retouching and varnishing was sufficient.[62] There is no reason to assume that the old varnish layer applied by Hulswit in 1817 was removed on this occasion.

In June 1845, Nicolaas Hopman again applied two layers of varnish to Rembrandt's canvas at Mazel's behest.[63] Varnishing and 'cleaning' appeared to have been almost annual events for the permanent restorer of the Mauritshuis.[64] Just what this signified was described by the director in 1850 on the occasion of a request from the National Gallery in London for information on the conservation of paintings. 'Except in the event of urgent cases, one limits oneself to cleaning the paintings once a year, for which a warm period in the middle of the summer is chosen, after the room has been cleaned. Subsequently, dark or dull paintings receive a more or less light varnish of mastic and in general one takes the opportunity to perform only those restorations that are strictly necessary.'[65]

> The unstable climate in the Mauritshuis will have been the reason why the paintings had to be 'cleaned' so often. As a result of the dry winters and humid summers the thick layers of varnish will have certainly sustained some bloom, craquelure and thereby blanching. With the application of the double varnish layer, the painting had at least four layers of varnish.

The lining of the *Anatomy Lesson of Dr Tulp* was not something Mazel dared trust to a Dutchman, as appears in his letter of 8 July 1846 to the minister of Internal Affairs.[66] Conversely, there were risks associated with allowing the capital canvas to be transported over the borders, and an impasse arose. In the meantime, foreign visitors to the museum noted the painting's poor condition and voiced their concern. For instance, in 1857 Maxime Ducamp published an extensive lament: 'Unfortunately, this splendid canvas is ill.' He spoke of flaking paint and traces of an old restoration (by Hulswit) which, according to him, looked like dried out boils, chiefly in the cadaver, the collar and the face of Tulp and in most of the portrait heads. He pleaded for new restoration.[67]

> The description 'dried out boils' appears somewhat exaggerated. However, what does seem certain is that a series of vertical, open cracks were visible, which even today can still be seen as a wide pattern of craquelure. Should the glue lining have been unable to keep the warped paint layer attached to the canvas in the damp Mauritshuis, which is likely, then the painting surely looked terrible in raking light.

Two years later, Mazel had still not overcome his reservations to having the *Anatomy Lesson of Dr Tulp* restored at home. In a letter of 29 June 1859 to the minister, Mazel noted that while he did occasionally allow Hopman to perform a relining, for Rembrandt's painting he wanted to invoke the help of the French painter Étienne le Roy (1828-after 1875), who was active in Brussels. The latter had also treated Rubens' altarpiece in the Cathedral in Antwerp, successfully according to the experts.[68] On 12 July 1859, Mazel informed Le Roy that he had received permission to have a relining done for the amount of 700 guilders. This was a friendly price and thus should not be voiced publicly. Heading the correspondence concerning this matter are the words 'Confidential' and 'Secret'.[69]

In August 1859, Le Roy travelled to The Hague to take delivery of the painting. The capital was to be deprived of its masterpiece for almost a year. The restoration proved very difficult, but little explanation for this was forthcoming from the Frenchmen.[70] In a letter dated 22 July 1860, Le Roy announced that he had finally put the finishing touches to the painting by Rembrandt. He had relined it, removed several layers of varnish and applied a fresh layer.[71] The reason he gave for the length of time it had taken him to perform the work had to do with the many retouchings.[72] In a lithograph by Ch. Binger, Le Roy indicated the places where he had applied these overpaintings.

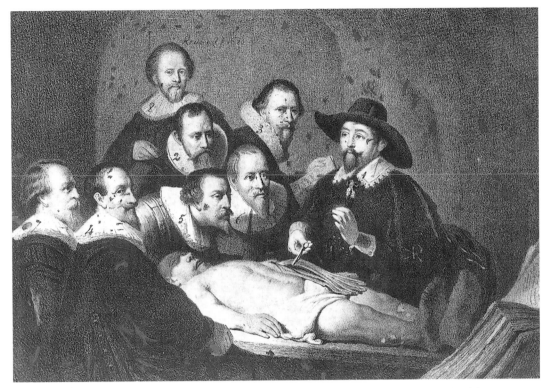

Mazel noted thereby: 'That marked in brown and yellow indicates the restoration realised by Mr Etienne Le Roy during the relining' (fig. 8). According to a caption by Le Roy himself, he had restored the fingers of no. 4, Adriaen Slabbraen.[73] With his request for payment of the stipulated honorarium, Mazel informed the minister that 'both the lining and the following treatment ... were highly satisfactory.'[74] Mazel even proposed the restorer as a candidate for 'the Cross of the order of the Oak Crown' for his superb work.[75]

The Mauritshuis' joy was short lived. Mazel asked Le Roy to come to The Hague in 1866 to look at the *Anatomy Lesson* because blisters had appeared in a few places.[76] Le Roy's answer was not forthcoming for the time being. In 1868, Mazel again informed Le Roy that fissures had been observed chiefly in the darker parts of the canvas and that paint was cupping in a few spots. The museum gallery had been cleaned, but without expert advice he dared not hang the painting.[77] In a reply, Le Roy placed the blame on previous restorers and noted that craquelure occurred in all of Rembrandt's paintings. As a remedy, he had cleaned the painting with a soft brush.[78] The restorer appears to have been prepared to travel to The Hague in April 1869, but this visit was postponed due to the illness of a child.[79] He probably did come and look at the painting in the end, for in a letter of January 1874 he told Mazel that he was 'particularly happy' that the painting was still in such excellent condition.

The white craquelure Mazel claimed had returned, primarily in the black coat of Dr Tulp, was explained by Le Roy as a phenomenon characteristic of Rembrandt and probably nothing more than dust. However, it is highly likely that this was drying cracks. This can still be discerned in Tulp's cloak, and elsewhere. The light ground or underpainting shines through the craquelure here and there.[80]

Museum Restorers and the Advent of the Natural Sciences (1877-1951)

With the dawn of the era of the large museum in the nineteenth century, the need for more specialised museum personnel able to preserve the collections slowly grew. Parallel to this development, several natural scientists took the initiative to investigate and bring out advice on new restoration techniques. Max von Pettenköfer introduced the use of the microscope in investigating paintings in 1870 (fig. 9); Oswald first used microchemistry in 1905; Faber initiated the use x-radiography for paintings and Kougel ultraviolet fluorescence in 1914; and infrared reflectography was applied at the end of the 1920s.

Willem Anthonie Hopman (1828-1910), the son of Nicolaas Hopman, distinguished himself from his predecessors as the first to apply the natural sciences to the field of restoration in the Netherlands. He maintained good contacts with the leading Berlin restorer Alois Hauser (1875-1919), who also treated paintings in the Mauritshuis.

9. The use of the microscope for the study of paintings was introduced in 1870.

From their very first meeting during Hopman's intership in Berlin, the two continued to exchange restoration techniques throughout their lives.[81] These new developments slowly also began to play a role in the restoration history of the *Anatomy Lesson of Dr Nicolaes Tulp*. Mazel's successor at the Mauritshuis, J.K.J. de Jonge (1828-1880), had been concerned about Rembrandt's *chef d'oeuvre* from the moment he took up his position in 1875. He informed the minister of this in a 'communication concerning the condition of painting no. 146,' to which he appended an extensive report by Hopman. He had posed this expert three questions: first, what did he think of the condition of the painting before 1860?; second, what had Le Roy done?; and third, what was needed to preserve the canvas for the future? The Amsterdam restorer's extensive answer also contained a clear judgement: the adhesion of the paint was particularly unstable; Le Roy should never have used water soluble elements for the lining; and the last lining should be removed immediately.[82]

Hopman deliberated on the future of the canvas, and upon new inspection told De Jonge that he would 'perform [a restoration] preferably entirely without remuneration.' After sending his equipment to The Hague with a bargeman, he was prepared to commence work in the Mauritshuis on 10 June 1877.[83] But first, the minister of Internal Affairs, Heemskerk, wanted to discuss the prospective restoration with Hopman. On 4 July he granted permission for the painting to be relined.[84] Hopman wrote that, 'Considering the painting's dangerous condition' he would work 'out of pure interest', thus free of charge, and only upon receipt of a written statement from the minister approving his restoration proposal. He considered himself capable in this area chiefly because of his familiarity with the painting's earlier condition and because he was the only restorer with 'chemical knowledge.' In the event of failure, Hopman wanted to prevent 'perhaps being the one blamed by posterity for damaging the painting out of ignorance.'[85]

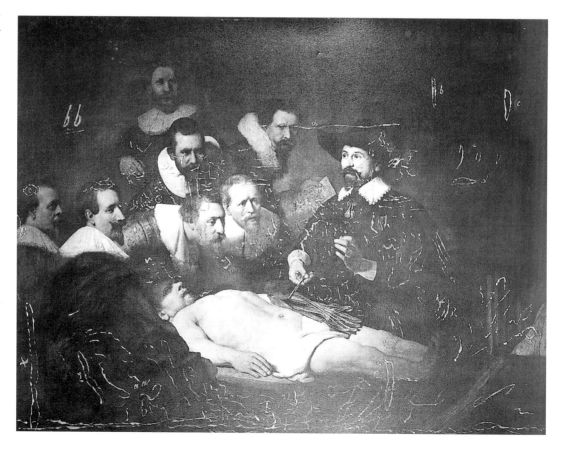

10. Photograph of the *Anatomy Lesson of Dr Nicolaes Tulp* with indications of the damaged areas by the restorer Willem Anthonie Hopman, 1877

On 20 July 1877, De Jonge sent the minister a photograph of the painting's condition before restoration.[86] On another print, Hopman indicated the damaged areas of the painting (fig. 10).[87] When the minister gave his permission a second time for relining on 31 July, Hopman had already been hard at work for ten days.[88] On 17 August, notice could be sent to the minister that 'Mr Hopman has this time again acquitted himself excellently of the difficult task.'[89] On 21 August 1877, Hopman submitted a statement for 32 days of living expenses with an assistant, wages for said assistant, and the costs of materials, including 'adhesive, canvas, two stretchers and a new canvas stretcher', totalling 1,340 guilders.[90] As early as 25 August 1877, *De Nederlandsche Spectator* was able to report that Hopman 'had acquitted himself of his task most excellently ... This is pure preservation. The dirt, the damage is removed, the paint layer firmly and smoothly attached to a new canvas, nothing is inpainted.'[91]

> For this fourth lining Hopman used his father's new wax-resin technique.[92] The wax-resin mixture recommended by Hopman consisted of three parts of colophony, four of white wax and two of Venice turpentine.[93] The wax-resin method was considered the ideal manner for impregnating and lining canvasses in countries with a damp climate, such as the Netherlands.[94]

In 1885 a new director was appointed to the Mauritshuis, the landscape painter Simon van den Berg (1812-1891), and W.A. Hopman was again invited to come to The Hague. '[I] hope to be at the Mauritshuis tomorrow [7 April] at ten o'clock in the morning', he telegrammed.[95] Two days later the director sent the ministry an estimate for the costs of lining six paintings and renewing the varnish of seven paintings, including Rembrandt's *Anatomy Lesson*.[96]

> It has long been suspected that in renewing the varnish, Hopman used copaiva balsam or alcohol vapours, that is to say that he worked according to Pettenköfer's regeneration method. Copaiva balsam was very popular among restorers at the end of the nineteenth and beginning of the twentieth century because it produced good results. The essential oils in copaiva balsam were thought to soften old varnish. And, by exposing the painting to alcohol vapours in a closed box at the same tim, the varnish would coalesce and the craquelure and dullness would be eliminated. The underlying idea was that this was a way to avoid using solvents for removing old varnish, thereby reducing to a minimum the risk of damaging the original material. However, today copaiva balsam has a bad name because it has been shown that in time it can penetrate the paint layer and affect its structure. However, no traces of this substance were detected in the *Anatomy Lesson* in a recent investigation.

By the time Van den Berg was succeeded by Abraham Bredius (1855-1946) in 1889, restoration of the varnish had become a routine job for Hopman. In 1891 he treated the *Anatomy Lesson of Dr Tulp* for a third time.[97] Bredius had the painting regenerated in 1906 and relined again in 1908. Both of these treatments were done by C.F.L. de Wild.

> It is not clear why the relining of 1877 was so quickly replaced. Many seventeenth-century paintings, including Vermeer's *View of Delft*,[98] still benefit from Hopman's skilful relining: the comment 'you do not remove a Hopman lining' has almost become an axiom. The material of this fifth (and to date last) relining consists chiefly of wax, with small amounts of a resin-like substance (see p. 53). De Wild (fig. 11) also removed a 'thick layer of discoloured varnish',[99] retouched the painting and applied a new protective layer. For this he used 'his own varnish' and not 'Hauser's,' as Bredius told sub-director Martin.[100] Can one assume from this that De Wild was conscious of the destructive influence of Hauser's copaiva balsam retaining varnish?[101]

11. C.F.L. de Wild in his studio, c. 1920

Already in 1918, the Mauritshuis' director Willem Martin wrote that two of the most important paintings by Holland's greatest master [Rembrandt], the *Anatomy Lesson of Dr Nicolaes Tulp* and the *Nightwatch*, were covered with thick layers of varnish, retouchings and overpaintings.[102] Should one clean the *Anatomy Lesson* down to the bottom layer of varnish, according to him a background with columns and arches in grey tints would emerge. More-over, the cloak of the man at the left would show up partly black and partly violet or brown, and the corpse of the dead man would no longer be yellow but a very realistic leaden grey.[103]

In 1925, D. de Wild removed several discoloured overpaintings replacing them with new ones.
The varnish, too, was 'restored', which was probably only in the form of selective cleaning so that the new retouching could be more easily applied.[104]

In 1940, Martin requested the ministry's permission to allow the restorer J.C. Traas to restore the *Anatomy Lesson*. Martin wrote that while the painting had been excellently lined by the late C.F.L. de Wild in 1908, the front had been in need of treatment for some time. Many darkened retouchings and dull spots could be observed and the many discoloured varnish layers spoiled the esthetic effect. The ministry acquiesced, but because of storage in special depots - successively in Paaslo and Maastricht - necessitated by the outbreak of the Second World War, treatment never took place.[105] In October 1942, the supervisor during this storage, H.P. Baard, informed Martin that the painting displayed 'two blisters in the upper right corner as a result of the old canvas separating from the new one, possibly due to moisture in the Maastricht basement. The canvas is coated with fluff from the flannel cover, directly on the painting. I have removed the worst, but have left untouched the stubborn, stuck-on bits.'[106] Martin replied a few days later that the blisters had been present for years and had not worsened. Further, he added: 'Fluff sticks to it [the painting] each time it is covered with a blanket. The reason for this is the varnish, which has never entirely dried.'[107] He reported that he planned to visit Paaslo with the restorer Traas to remove the fluff from the canvas.

The paintings in hiding returned to their 'stable' in 1945.[108] Probably in connection with a new installation of the museum they had to be made presentable, and in 1946 Traas removed the top layer of varnish and several overpaintings from the *Anatomy Lesson*.[109] Five years later the painting was again in need of urgent restoration, which was also performed by Traas. Once more, overpaintings were removed and retouchings applied. The *Annual Report* of 1951 includes an extensive description of the final result: 'All manner of details have clearly emerged. A surprise is that another signature on an old layer of varnish was painted over the original signature on the wall, which has now vanished entirely. Old overpaintings, most of them far too copious and coarsely done, could be refined.
It was also clear that the young artist [Rembrandt] had wrestled with his difficult commission. Numerous pentimenti show how he sometimes shifted figures a few centimetres. The cadaver has a sensitive and in no way harsh colour, and also far more colour has appeared in the heads and the clothing of the man. Without exaggeration it may be said that we now once again own the masterpiece by the young Rembrandt.'[110]

III The Restoration of the *Anatomy Lesson of Dr Nicolaes Tulp*

Petria Noble and Jørgen Wadum

Rembrandt's *Anatomy Lesson of Dr Nicolaes Tulp* was previously restored in 1951. It was essentially the degradation of the secondary materials used in the previous restoration, such as the varnish and retouchings, that after only forty years, made the painting difficult to appreciate. The retouchings, which when first applied no doubt perfectly matched the original paint, had discoloured and the varnish had yellowed as well (fig. 1). Therefore, in 1994 it was decided to restore the painting in order to improve its aesthetic appearance.

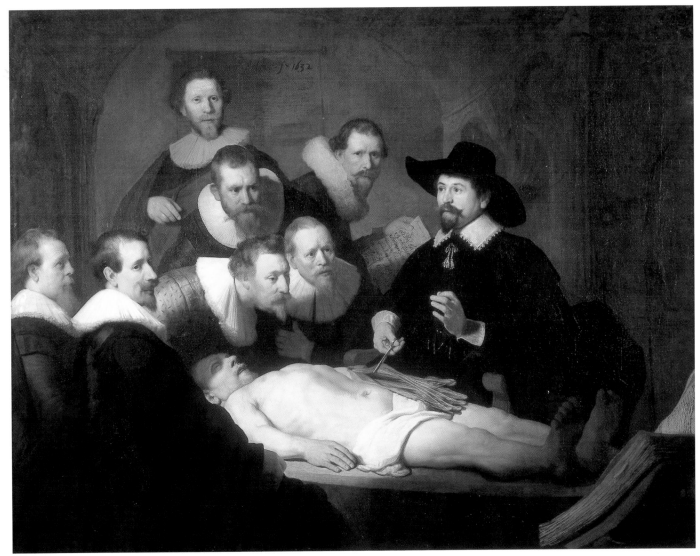

1. *The Anatomy Lesson of Dr Nicolaes Tulp* before the present restoration, 1996

The aim of the restoration, to be completed in September 1998, was to ensure that the intention of Rembrandt was honoured, particularly in the light of the painting's long history.
The removal of the yellowed varnish and the discoloured and excessively large retouchings and fillings restored the dramatic colour values of the painting and revealed many details previously obscured. With the reconstruction of lost or damaged areas of paint a careful balance has been struck between what was desired and what is acceptable in a restoration. After all, the group portrait is 366 years old and has suffered in the past. Now, for the first time in many years, the painting is closer to what it must have looked like when the surgeons saw it hanging on the wall of their guild chamber in 1632.

Below is a description of the treatment and a presentation of the facts established in the technical examination of the painting - initiated already as early as 1996 - followed by an essay on Rembrandt's painting technique used in the *Anatomy Lesson of Dr Nicolaes Tulp*.

1 The Condition

Research Methods

In the first phase of the research the painting was examined, initially with the naked eye in normal and raking light, then with the stereomicroscope, and finally with special techniques, using ultraviolet light, infra-red photography and reflectography as well as x-radiography. Other Rembrandt paintings from the 1630s were studied for comparison. Cross sections were prepared from tiny samples of paint, which provided valuable information about the build-up and the thickness of the original paint layers, the varnish and overpaint. Minuscule paint samples were also studied with highly sophisticated analytical techniques by scientists at the ICN (Dutch Institute for Cultural Heritage) and the FOM Institute for Atomic and Molecular Physics/MOLART to investigate the structure and composition of different parts of the painting. This was done in order to have a better understanding of the chemical and physical interactions of the proposed solvent to be used on the original paint. When the cleaning process had been completed, questions focused on learning more about Rembrandt's painting technique. In every phase, the greatest care was taken to assess the analytical results in the light of the factual evidence provided by the painting and historical information from the archives.

The Canvas

The painting has been lined five times in all; before 1877 it was paste-lined three times. In 1877 and 1908 it was lined with wax/resin and further impregnated with wax in the 1930s. Although by today's standards such treatments involving high levels of heat, moisture and pressure are considered extreme, these methods were quite acceptable at the time. Certainly the effect these treatments have had on the painting is visible in the painting's surface(fig. 2). Much of the original paint has been flattened. Pronounced vertical cracks, some with raised edges, and others where the paint is overlapping and flattened, indicate shrinking and expansion of the canvas as a result of excessive moisture. Deformation has occurred, as is illustrated by the large losses along the lower edge of the painting when the painting was lined without the losses being filled.

However, the canvas is structurally in good condition; the present double wax/resin lining was applied in 1908 by the then restorer, C.F.L. de Wild Sr. The thick and irregular appearance of the lining material on the back of the canvas, however, is not consistent with the usually thin, smooth appearance of the lining material normally seen in De Wild's linings. It was furthermore significant

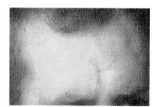

2. The wrinkled paint structure on Jacob Block's forehead was probably caused by excessive moisture and heat employed in the lining of the painting.

3. The back of the painting in ultraviolet illumination. The patchy appearance was caused by later impregnation with wax, which occurred between 1920 and 1940, as well as by the local treatment in the upper and lower left from 1942.

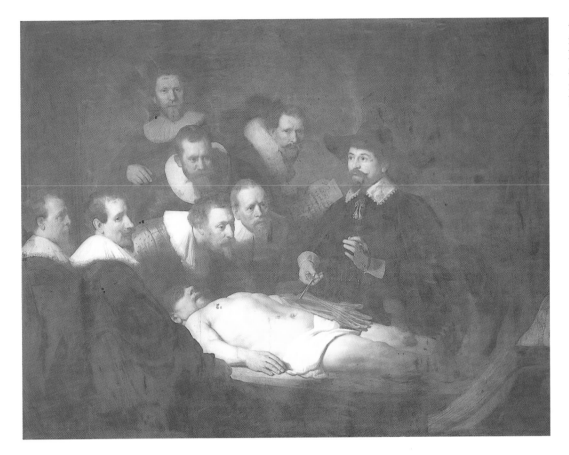

that in numerous samples analysed, only beeswax with the addition of some paraffin was identified.[1] For comparison, samples from four other paintings, documented as having been lined by De Wild between 1901 and 1908, were analysed and in each case a typical mixture of beeswax and diterpenoid resin (probably colophony) was identified. It could also be seen that the painting had been removed from the stretcher after the lining in 1908, which supported the idea that the entire canvas had been impregnated with the wax/paraffin mixture in order to reinforce De Wild's lining from 1908. This must have taken place in the period between 1920 and 1940 (fig. 3).[2] Despite references to the use of copaïva balsam in the restoration reports of W.A. Hopman and De Wild, there were no visual indications such as displaced paint or softened cracks. Nor could any trace of copaïva balsam be detected from the numerous samples analysed (see p. 49).

The Varnish

Research into the yellowed mastic varnish applied by Traas in the 1951 restoration yielded surprising results. The varnish was extremely uneven in thickness, varying between 10 and 75 microns (1 micron = 0.001 mm).[3] In general, three layers of varnish were detected. In the background under the three layers of varnish, a thin resinous overpaint and another layer of varnish were found (fig. 4). The total thickness of the varnish layers and the overpaint in this area was 75 microns. In contrast, the thickness of the varnish on Dr Tulp's cloak was 10 microns. The presence of common turpentine, or Venice Turpentine, and beeswax in the varnish was probably the result of residual material from the solvent used in the 1951 varnish or from residual material from regenerations or linings that were not completely removed in the past. It was also found that the varnish on the corpse contained black and red pigments; tinted varnishes were often applied in the past to imitate old varnishes. Although the debate about the over-cleaning of paintings was probably an important issue for Traas in 1951, it is unlikely that he applied a toned varnish to the lit areas for fear that the painting would be considered over-cleaned. It is more likely that it was applied for aesthetic reasons 'to prevent the brilliance of the colours from offending the eye.'[4]

5. On the x-radiograph mosaic losses in the original paint appear dark.

6. The small greyish patches in the centre of the x-radiograph detail indicate loss of surface paint due to blisters from heat damage that occurred in the early eighteenth century.

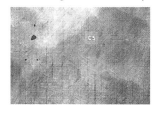

Losses

The losses in the original paint down to the canvas are clearly visible in the x-ray mosaic (fig. 5). The largest losses are found in the lower 25 cm of the painting. Also worth mentioning are a series of smaller losses in a vertical formation just to the right of Tulp's face and in Colevelt and Slabbraen's suits. These losses are considered to have occurred in the late eighteenth or early nineteenth century due to moisture and water damage from the poor conditions in which the painting was hung (see p. 40). The jagged, irregular contours of the losses seem to be associated with flaking, as a result of moisture damage. It is unlikely that they resulted - as De Vries suggested in 1978 - from the painting's exposure to the fire in the guild chamber in 1723.[5] If this were true, the dark paint next to the losses in the foreground would also show evidence of heat damage. In fact, only in a few places in the painting could damage be attributed to heat. In the upper part of the painting some localised areas of wrinkled and matt paint appear to be the result of heat damage, though probably caused by hot irons used in past linings. In comparison with the other anatomy lesson paintings which were hanging in the guild chamber at the time of the 1723 fire in which a few were badly damaged (see p. 33), only the small superficial losses on the right side of Tulp's cloak are comparable with the losses resulting from blisters, as seen for example in the badly damaged *Anatomy Lesson of Dr Jan Deijman* (p. 24, fig. 16). On the other hand, these could also have been caused by the so-called 'fiery smoke' from 1732 (fig. 6).

Abrasion

The extent of abrasion and overpaint was more difficult to assess due to the discoloured and fractured varnish. Examination in ultra-violet light indicated extensive overpainting in a thin glaze-like paint over the architecture in the background. Cross sections revealed that over the dark grey original paint of the background was a dark resinous layer, applied between varnish layers. However, it was not clear what the overpaint was covering as no damage could be discerned on the x-ray. In this context, caution was exercised in attributing the somewhat abraded appearance of the figures deepest in the background, Hartmansz and Van Loenen, to wear rather than to Rembrandt's deliberately thin and sketchy handling of the paint in achieving 'aerial perspective' in the painting. [6] The latter proved to be the case when the background was cleaned. Also the background figures, which in the past had been described as abraded, appeared to be essentially intact.

Overpaint

Even with the naked eye a distinct difference is noticeable between Nicolaes Tulp's jacket and those of the other doctors. Tulp's black jacket, according to a document dated 20 September 1732, was so badly damaged by hot smoke from a chimney that it blistered and had to repaired (see p. 40). Examination of cross sections indicated that under the overpaint a thick layer of bone black constituting the original paint of the jacket was intact. Two applications of overpaint were evident: the first, a thin layer of bone black, was probably applied in the early eighteenth century, given the fact that the ageing cracks seen in this layer correspond with the craquelure of the underlying paint. [7] A later, thin resinous overpaint was applied in the previous restoration of 1951 (fig. 7).

Fillings

Many fillings applied to the losses on the painting were very disturbing, in most cases too high and too large, extending more than one centimetre over the original paint. The overpaint, in addition to being discoloured, was also considered too crude and in general greatly disturbed the reading of the picture. Study of the losses indicated fillings from four previous restorers who treated the painting: whitish chalk (Traas, 1951), a second chalk filling (D. de Wild, 1925), a brown waxy material (C.F. de Wild, 1908), and a coarse brown oil paint, possibly a palette scraping (W.A. Hopman, 1877).

7. Cross section of paint from Tulp's jacket in ultraviolet illumination. The oldest overpaint runs into a crack in the original paint; the resinous layer between the fluorescing varnish layers is the overpaint applied in the 1951 restoration.

Retouching

Traas's linseed oil retouchings from 1951, apart from being rather crude and larger than necessary, were discoloured. Those containing lead white and zinc white had turned whitish [blanched], while the dark retouchings had generally become darker(figs 8 and 9). [8] With the light retouchings the degradation is due to the breakdown of the oil medium by basic pigments, such as lead white and zinc white, and in the case of darkened retouches because of darkening of the large amount of oil absorbed by dark earth pigments.

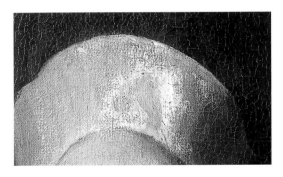

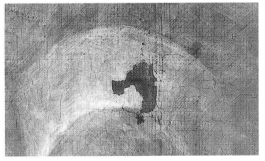

<< 8. Nicolaes Tulp's right-hand cuff with discoloured [blanched] retouching

< 9. Nicolaes Tulp's right-hand cuff, where it can be seen that the actual paint loss is much smaller than the retouching (detail of the x-radiograph)

Names and Numbers added later

Alongside every portrait is a painted number which corresponds with a number and a name on the sheet of paper held by Hartman Hartmansz. These additions were mentioned for the first time in around 1750. The spelling of the names - Blok instead of Block, Kalkoen instead of Calkoen - points to a dating not earlier than 1675. [9] Because more Amsterdam anatomy lesson paintings contain similar inscriptions, it is not unthinkable that they were applied during the great restoration campaign of 1732. [10]

55

Cross sections of the paint build-up of the numbers and names were taken to see if any evidence could substantiate their application at a later date. The presence of a very old varnish layer in between the background paint and that of the letters and numbers indicates that they were applied long after the painting was completed and varnished (figs 10 and 11). The added list of names obscures an original part of the painting, an anatomical sketch of an outstretched arm Rembrandt made on the sheet of paper (see p. 22).

10. The number '7' above Jacob Colevelt, applied in the early eighteenth century

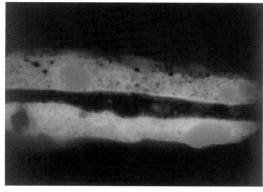

11. Cross section from the number '7' in ultraviolet illumination
An old thin varnish layer is visible between the paint of the background and the number. Lower ground is missing from sample.

In the 1951 restoration Traas reconstructed the somewhat fragmentary light grey inscription with dark paint (fig. 12), which severely distorts the spatial illusion in the picture, especially since the other texts in the painting - that of the open book in the foreground and the text on the scroll on the wall in the background - were not intended to be legible. Therefore it was decided that Traas's reconstruction should be removed so that the anatomical drawing below and the fragmentary eighteenth century remains could be made visible. The numbers beside the figures are well preserved, though not distracting, and were left untouched.

12. The anatomical drawing in Hartman Hartmansz's hand before restoration

An unusual Surface Phenomenon

During the extensive technical research of Rembrandt paintings in the Mauritshuis in the 1970s seventies W. Froentjes correctly observed small crater-like holes over the entire surface of the painting.[11] Although their diameter of between 100 and 200 microns makes the phenomenon difficult to discern with the naked eye, there was concern that the holes could function as tunnels for solvent during the cleaning (fig. 13). The phenomenon was subsequently extensively studied.

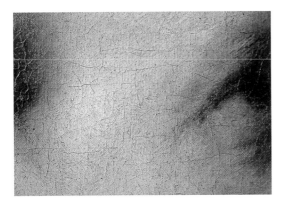

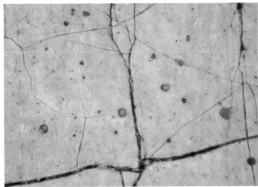

13. Detail of Jacob Colevelt's face with numerous inclusions/holes in the paint layer.

14. Microphotograph of the inclusions/holes in the flesh paint. The holes, where the inclusions were lost, were subsequently filled with darkened varnish.

Froentjes argued that the holes must have formed within one hundred years after the completion of the painting as a result of the painting's early exposure to heat. The round form of the holes is completely regular. A ring of blanching was observed in the varnish above the hole. Small dots of blanching were also observed in other places of the varnish layer, probably corresponding to underlying inclusions not broken through. It was observed that many of the holes contain a whitish spherical inclusion which protrudes upwards through the paint layer (fig. 14). The phenomenon is not colour dependent, but is most pronounced in the thinner, dark areas. The inclusions are less radio-absorbent than the surrounding paint, and are visible on the x-ray as small dark spots confirming their presence below the thickly applied lead white areas where in many cases they have not broken through the surface.

The cause of these holes/inclusions was attributed by Froentjes to the painting's early exposure to the 1723 fire, where it was hypothesised that organic fractions in the not completely polymerised painting had been volatised through the surface of the painting. However, if it were indeed due to heat, the darker passages of the painting should show plastic deformation since they are more readily affected by heat than other areas. In addition, the phenomenon has recently been observed in many seventeenth century paintings by a number of artists from diverse collections. Also, in some paintings the phenomenon only appears in areas containing white. The widespread presence of this phenomenon would exclude any relation to environmental factors and past restoration treatments. Finally, analyses of the inclusions revealed a possible, albeit complex solution to the problem. The study of cross sections showed that the inclusions have a round, ball shape and that they are

15. Cross section of an inclusion in the paint from Jacob Colevelt's face showing its origin in the second, grey ground The inclusion consists of saponified lead compounds. It is also interesting to note that the flesh paint is applied directly over the double ground.

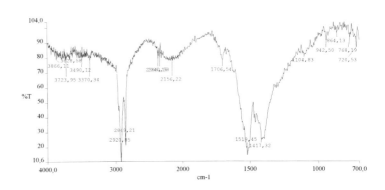

situated in the essentially lead white second ground layer (fig. 15). An isolated inclusion analysed with FTIR showed absorption bands comparable to that of a lead soap, such as lead stearate (fig. 16).[12] XRD demonstrated the presence of a large quantity of lead chloride hydroxide (Fiedlerite) in the inclusions and to a lesser extent in the second groundlayer. Although a naturally occurring mineral, it is thought to be present as a reaction product, and is possibly formed by a combination of the

16. FTIR spectrum of an isolated inclusion compares well with a reference spectrum of lead stearate.

purification of the linseed oil binding medium with salt and drying with red lead.[13] Although still somewhat hypothetical, we do know that the inclusions were formed by the agglomeration and saponification of lead compounds within the ground layer, their increased volume causing them to 'erupt' through the thin paint layer. In most cases the inclusions were finally abraded or lost during the numerous earlier treatments of the painting resulting in only the remaining crater-like hole. The holes in the paint layer are thus nothing other than the voids left from the loss of inclusions. Many holes were filled with secondary substances, such as darkened varnish, and therefore appear dark, while others have been abraded, resulting in a flatter surface profile with a more irregular shape.[14]

The concern that the holes would function as tunnels for the solvent during cleaning was thus found to be ungrounded. From studying the appearance, yet another conclusion can be deduced. The fact that the inclusions, or holes are generally only found locally suggests that for the particular area a different paint was made, using specific oil for that particular pigment. In the case of the *Anatomy Lesson of Dr Nicolaes Tulp* this was oil purified with salt water and then dried. This is significant in that it supports recent theories that Dutch seventeenth-century artists, made their paint anew for different parts of the painting using specific oils and dryers, depending on the pigment used.[15]

Conclusion

The research conducted into the condition of the painting led to the conclusion that the proposed cleaning of the *Anatomy Lesson of Dr Nicolaes Tulp* was not only technically feasible, but quite straightforward. The still young varnish, in this case a mastic varnish not even fifty years old, is much more soluble than the 366-year old oxidised linseed oil paint. As a rule, a solvent mixture is used for the removal of natural resin varnishes, which in practice means finding the correct proportion between an inactive, non-polar and an active, polar solvent.[16] Cleaning tests resulted in choosing a combination of iso-octane and ethanol.[17]

2 The Treatment

Varnish Removal

The varnish was carefully removed using cotton swabs and the chosen solvent mixture, usually with the aid of either the stereomicroscope or a head magnifier. As anticipated, there was no difficulty in removing the 46-year-old mastic varnish; in areas where the unevenly applied varnish was thicker a slightly more polar variant of the solvent mixture was used, followed by a slightly less polar one as the original surface of the painting became exposed. Very little older varnish had been left on the painting by previous restorers; only in the interstices, such as in the scratched lines in the book and in deep cuppings of paint were embrowned varnish remains observed.

Visually, the lightest areas are altered most by a discoloured varnish, and only after its removal did the fine, careful modelling and colour nuances of the five foremost figures of Tulp, Slabbraen, De Wit, Block and Calkoen - as well as the corpse - become visible (fig. 17). The excellent state of preservation of the lit areas, the faces and collars - despite the numerous cleanings and linings - is due largely to Rembrandt's opaque paint mixtures. In these figures the lights and highlights were worked more directly into the paint, whereas in the figures further away (Van Loenen, Hartmansz and Colevelt), the warm lights were mostly added on top of thinner, more summarily painted flesh layers.

17. Adriaen Slabbraen's head during varnish removal.

The cleaning of the dark jackets of Colevelt and Slabbraen at the left of the picture showed the highly obscuring effect of the degraded varnish over the black paint (fig. 18). During cleaning, brownish, grey and purplish tints became visible in the lit areas of the jackets, better preserved because of the admixture of lead white in the paint (fig. 19). In comparison, the thinner, blacker/darker areas of the jackets show some wear, which to a large extent had been thinly glazed over by Traas in the previous restoration, probably with the intention of integrating the two large restored losses in this area.

18. Jacob Colevelt and Adriaen Slabbraen, before cleaning

19. Jacob Colevelt and Adriaen Slabbraen, after removal of varnish and overpaint

20. The red glaze on the back of the chair in ultraviolet illumination Painted in organic red lake, it has a characteristic orange fluorescence.

A remarkable thick red glaze, not previously mentioned, also came to light on the back and seat of Slabbraen's chair (fig. 20).

Removal of Overpaint and Fillings

Many areas, particularly the background, the book in the lower right-hand corner and the damaged lower edge, were covered with thin resinous overpaint. Before removal of the varnish it was difficult to judge whether the overpaint covered abrasion. Photographs of the painting, taken in the late nineteenth and early twentieth centuries, although of high quality were of little help in assessing the condition, as in most cases the backgrounds of the photographs had been artistically manipulated. Nor was there any indication of damage in the background in the photographs taken before and during Traas's restoration in 1951. Therefore, once the varnish and overpaint had been removed, not entirely surprisingly a sketchily painted background was revealed, quite similar to the upper right-hand background in the *Portrait of Johannes Wtenbogaert* (Amsterdam, Rijksmuseum), also from 1632. This led to the conclusion that in the previous restoration Rembrandt's intended sketchiness had been misinterpreted as abrasion, as a result of which the thinner passages were overpainted. The thin abraded dark layer representing the stack of books in the lower right-hand corner and the damaged bottom edge were also liberally glazed over in a translucent paint. In the 1950s this was a not unusual solution to integrate damages and abrasion, but by today's standards it is unacceptable.

Indeed it seems that the lower edge had probably been obscured by successive campaigns of filling and overpainting for a much longer time (centuries). An engraving by J.P. de Frey, made in 1798 after the *Anatomy Lesson of Dr Nicolaes Tulp* (fig. 21) depicts the lower edge as a featureless area in comparison with the highly detailed background. Study of the 'after-cleaning' photograph taken in 1951 led to the conclusion that Traas had left many retouchings and fillings from restorations prior to 1951. Rather than removing the old fillings he chose to obscure them with copious glazing and overpainting. Fortunately, although bound with linseed oil, the retouchings and overpaint were still quite soluble and could be removed along with the varnish.

21. J.P. Frey.
The Anatomy Lesson of Dr Nicolaes Tulp
Amsterdam, Rijksmuseum

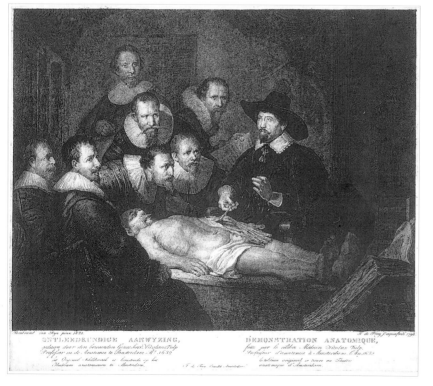

Tulp's jacket was the most puzzling area of the painting, especially given the document from 1732 pertaining to the damage to and the repainting of the jacket (see p. 40). After varnish removal, Rembrandt's reworking of the background over the cloak was easily recognisable along the top-right contour of the cloak. In most of the jacket, however, opaque and even handling of the paint with little definition suggested that the jacket was to some extent obscured with an early overpaint. Cross-sectional analysis indicated that the original paint of the jacket was intact, and that it was covered (in most places) with either one or two thin layers of overpaint (see fig. 7).[18] Given the absence of an intervening varnish below the first overpaint (seen in the cross section), and the insolubility of this layer, it was decided to remove only the recent overpaint in the chest and on the right-hand side of the cloak.

As described earlier, fillings from the previous four restorations were identified in losses along the lower edge (see p. 55). Although the fillings from 1951 were stable, they were too high, and in most cases larger than necessary, and were either reduced or removed (figs 22 and 23).

The three underlying fillings were only removed where they covered the original paint.[19] The earliest of the fillings was found to be extremely hard and insoluble, which necessitated softening with an acetone-gel followed by time-consuming, mechanical removal under the binocular microscope.[20]

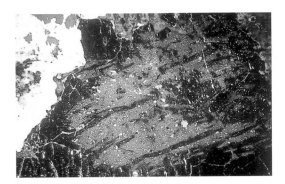

22. A filling in the lower part of the painting. The white chalk is from the 1951 restoration, the brown oil paint filling seen to go over the original paint was applied by W.A. Hopman in 1877.

23. Detail of loss in Adriaen Slabbraen's cloak, during varnish removal Here two campaigns of filling and retouching were found.

The size of the actual loss of the original paint was easily seen on the x-ray and could be constantly compared with the progress of cleaning on the painting itself. With the removal of the fillings, many previously overpainted details were brought into focus, especially the carved pedestal support of the table, which is not unlike that depicted in the engraving by Andries Stock (see p. 12, fig. 5)'.

After removal of varnish, overpaint and fillings it could be concluded that the painting, despite damage and successive restorations, is relatively well-preserved (fig. 24). In spite of several impregnations of the ground with materials used in the lining of the painting, the overall tonality of the painting does not seem to have altered visually. Only in the thin dark passages, such as the hair,

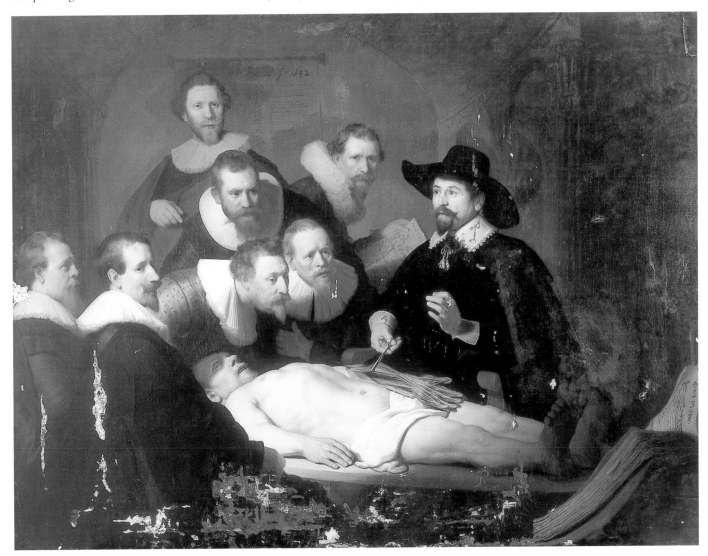

some parts of the costumes, the back of the book and parts of the background where the paint consists mainly of a single layer, was the painting found to be worn. Also, the bright highlights, the red of the chair and the purple of De Wit's suit have darkened and discoloured. The more pastose lit

24. *The Anatomy Lesson of Dr. Nicolaes Tulp*, after varnish removal

areas, such as the portraits, collars and the corpse of Aris Kint, are in an excellent state of preservation. Also, Rembrandt's signature was found to be in good condition (fig. 25).[21] Despite the paintings' dramatic past, we can therefore still appreciate Rembrandt's handling of the paint, as well as the dramatic contrast and deep chiaroscuro of the composition.

Retouching

After cleaning, an isolating brush coat of dammar varnish was applied to the painting, which after discussion with scientists and colleagues was considered to be the best choice because of its handling, good saturation and known solubility parameters.[22] The varnish saturates the painting so that the colours are clearly visible during the retouching phase; it also serves as an isolating layer between the original paint and the retouching in order to avoid the new materials being applied directly on the original paint surface.

25. The signature and date

Where possible, the pre-existing fillings were kept. Superficial losses were filled with a proprietary filler chosen for its flexibility, ease of handling and long-term solubility.[23] Prior to use, the filler was toned with dry pigments to approximate the colour of the grey ground. Where necessary, the fillings were textured by applying the filler with a small brush, or by carving the surface to imitate the cracks in the surrounding original paint.

This procedure was, however, not applicable for areas of large losses at the lower edge. Since successful retouching over large damages often depends on the success of the underlying filling in imitating the original paint, the surface texture for these areas was reproduced using a mould taken from a nearby area on the painting. Moulds were made using a dental silicone chosen for its ability to give good surface texture.[24] The mould was pressed into the newly applied filling in the loss, applying slight pressure to make an imprint of the original paint surface with all its cracks and irregularities.[25] Unlike previous restorations, the filling of losses was limited to precisely the size of the loss.

Since the goal of the restoration was to achieve an aesthetic reconstruction of the painting, deceptive retouching was chosen to compensate for the losses. Areas of lost original paint were first laid in with a flat, even layer of water colour to imitate the grey ground, followed by retouching with stable synthetic resin[26] and dry pigments for the main paint layer. Unlike oil paint, the composition of this paint is such that the retouchings will show little or no discoloration in the future.[27]

After cleaning, the eighteenth-century addition of the list of names over the anatomical drawing in the hand of Hartman Hartmansz. appeared vague and highly fragmentary (fig. 26). In order to preserve Rembrandt's spatial illusion it was decided not to reconstruct the names again.

After retouching, a final layer of dammar varnish was applied in order to protect and further saturate the picture (fig. 27). An ultra violet light inhibitor, *Tinuvin 292,* was added to the varnish, which in combination with a UV filtered environment has proven to dramatically slow down the yellowing and oxidation of the natural resin varnish.[28] The use of stable materials in the restoration, as well as the optimal display conditions in the museum, ensure that the frequency of the cleaning cycle of the painting will be greatly extended. Since the first documented restoration in 1700 and the previous one in 1951, treatment occurred on average every 13 years.

26. The anatomical drawing after varnish removal

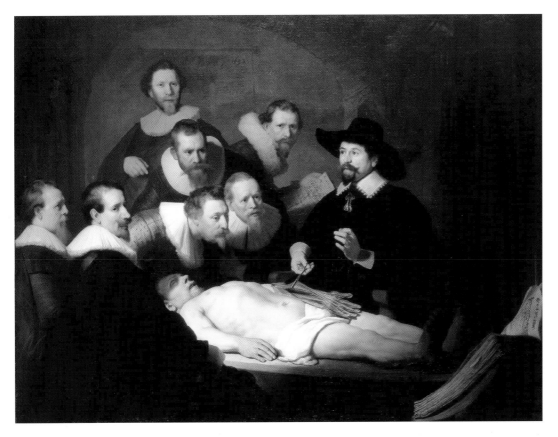

27. *The Anatomy Lesson of Dr. Nicolaes Tulp* after completion of the restoration

The Frame

There is no documentation pertaining to the frame the painting had before 1875. In that year, Carel Vosmaer described the painting as having 'a black frame (made by Mr. Laarman) surrounded by a green curtain'. Corresponding to Vosmaer's description, a painting by A. F. Heijligers from 1884 depicts the *Anatomy Lesson of Dr Nicolaes Tulp* with a black frame hanging against a green curtain. Until now the current frame was mahogany in colour with an oil-gilded inner profile. Since the design and scale seem appropriate for the picture, it was decided not to replace the frame. Adjustments were made to the colour to restore its black appearance,[29] more in keeping with frames of the seventeenth century, which simultaneously confers more depth to the painting.

3. Rembrandt's Painting Technique in the *Anatomy Lesson of Dr Nicolaes Tulp*

The restoration of a painting offers the rare opportunity to examine an artist's painting technique in great detail. The removal of secondary material, such as discoloured varnish, retouching and excess filling, allows a closer look at areas that were obscured for a long time. By combining visual examination with the stereomicroscope with a variety of analytical methods, such as the study of paint cross sections, new light can be shed on Rembrandt's technique and the materials used in the creation of the painting. During the restoration of the *Anatomy Lesson of Dr Nicolaes Tulp* much time was devoted to compiling technical information.

The Ground

The *Anatomy Lesson of Dr Nicolaes Tulp,* which essentially maintains its original format, was painted on a single, large piece of plain weave linen.[30] After stretching onto a strainer, the canvas was probably first prepared with a layer of glue-size which was followed by the application of a double ground. The double ground in the *Anatomy Lesson of Dr Nicolaes Tulp* is comparable with those on other paintings by Rembrandt and his contemporaries.[31] The first reddish ground layer is composed of red ochre, umber, and a little lead white.[32] This was applied with a primer's knife, which left long, curved scratches/indentations on the surface, which were subsequently filled with the lead-containing second ground (figs 28 and 29). Due to the x-ray absorbency of lead compounds, the indentations are visible on the x-radiograph as white lines. The second, grey ground consists mostly of lead white with a small amount of lamp black and a trace amount of yellow ochre.[33] In cross section the layer appears unusually transparent.[34]

∨ 28. A 'primer's knife' as illustrated in the De Mayerne manuscript. This is comparable with the one used for applying the red ground.

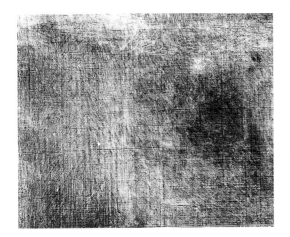
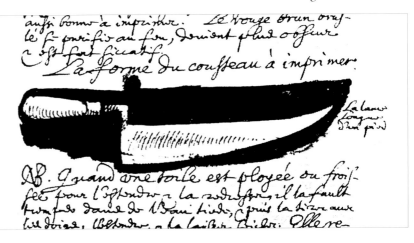

The Binding Medium

Over the past years paint samples from numerous paintings by Rembrandt and his school have been subjected to various analytical techniques in order to identify the type of oil and possible additives used.[35] From this research it has been established that Rembrandt and the painters of his time primarily used linseed oil as the binding medium in their paint. In the *Anatomy Lesson of Dr Nicolaes Tulp*, analysis demonstrated that Rembrandt used a non-heat bodied linseed oil,[36] probably purified according to a method described by Dr Théodore Turquet de Mayerne (1573-1655), in his manuscript entitled *Pictoria Sculptoria & quae subalternarum*, compiled between 1620 and 1646.[37] The process consisted of pressing the raw oil out of the linseeds, which was then purified and bleached by washing it in water. Materials such as sawdust, breadcrumbs, and lead powder were added to the water to absorb the plant mucilage and lecithin. This mixture would be left in the sun for 45 days, during which it was stirred five or six times a day.[38] Minute wood fibres have been observed embedded in the paint, indicating that the oil used in the painting was probably purified in this manner. The identification of lead chloride hydroxide in the grey ground, an interesting discovery in connection with the phenomenon of the holes in the paint layer, can possibly be explained as a reaction product, caused by the combination of purifying the oil with salt water and drying with the addition of red lead (see p. 57-58). These processes were described by De Mayerne: '…Take some rain water and dissolve some salt in it. Mix it with your oil … and shake it well and long several times for two or three days … let the salt water out and add a new [solution of water and salt] and repeat this procedure 12 to 15 times … After this wash the oil 3 to 4 times with rain water' (in translation).[39]

< 29. Detail of the x-radiograph. Indentations left by the knife when the ground was applied are visible as white curved lines on the x-ray.

> 30. Cross section of an inclusion from the paint of the background The darkish yellow area is the inclusion, within which particles of red lead were found.

>> 31. Backscattered electron image of the same cross section. The entire inclusion appears light, indicating the presence of lead compounds. This indicates that the red particles are also a lead compound.

The addition of red lead was demonstrated in numerous cross sections by the analysis of the red pigment particles observed only inside the inclusions in the second ground (figs 30 and 31).[40] De Mayerne's description for drying the oil is as follows: 'Grind red lead [minium] with oil … makes a strong siccative; if you mix a little [red lead] with [red] lake or vermilion it will make it dry quicker' (in translation).[41] The addition of gum was detected by FTIR in the binding medium of the thick red glaze used for the back and seat of the chair on which the most forefront figure is seated (figs 32 and 33). Since it would be necessary to apply the glaze thickly in order to achieve a strong red

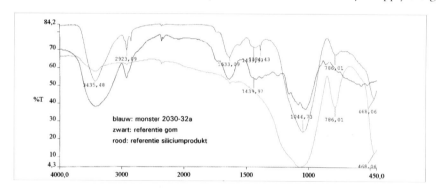

33. The FTIR spectrum of the red glaze is comparable with a reference spectrum of gum. Rembrandt mixed the gum with the oil to make an emulsion paint.

32. Cross section of the red glaze from the chair in the foreground. The red is built up in two layers. The lowest opaque layer is composed of red and black pigments, over which a thick translucent layer of organic red, containing a small addition of lead white, black, ochre and vermilion was applied.

colour, the addition of gum to the oil would have formed an emulsion resulting in better drying properties for a thick paint layer.

Dead-Colouring

Over the grey ground Rembrandt applied the sketchy dead-colouring, a monochrome undermodelling in translucent brown (fig. 34). In this phase, the painting would have looked something like the *Concord of the State* from 1642 (fig. 35). Cross sections demonstrate that the dead-colouring is found only in the shadow and dark areas of the faces, Tulp's (here in a very thin layer) and Matthijs Calkoen's suits and in the area where Hartman Hartmansz was originally positioned. In cross section the dead-colouring layer appears a semi-transparent reddish brown, rich in binding medium, comparing well to a reference sample of Cologne earth.[42] Contrary to earlier analysis, black pigments were not detected in this layer.[43] Only in Jacob Jansz. Colevelt, the figure at the far left, were black and a small amount of organic red found in addition to Cologne earth (fig. 36). This may suggest that this figure, previously thought to be a later addition, was added at a later stage of the undermodelling, and thus applied with a different paint mixture than the other figures (see p. 70-71).

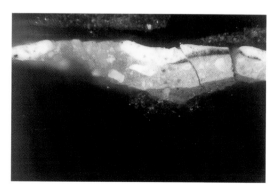

In the literature it has been stated that Rembrandt used translucent brown undermodelling in his panels, often in combination with a yellowish ground, and that in his canvas paintings he mostly used black for the undermodelling.[44] A brown undermodelling is encountered on a number of canvases created around 1630,[45] including the present painting. This is also found in later paintings on panel, as well as on canvas, suggesting that the choice of colour for the undermodelling was more dependent on the colour of the ground than on the type of support.

35. Rembrandt van Rijn
The Concord of the State
Panel, 74.6 x 101 cm
Rotterdam, Museum
Boijmans Van Beuningen

The First Paint Layers
After the dead-colouring was finished, Rembrandt started 'laying in' different areas in the painting, probably beginning with the grey-brown background. As this layer contains a substantial amount of lead white it is visible on the x-ray. Broadly painted with pronounced diagonal brushstrokes, spaces were left open for where the figures would be painted. The wall behind the figures in the centre is painted in grey, solid tones containing more lead white compared to the sketchy warm, dark earth tones of the extreme left and right-hand corners. The vigorous, loose brushstrokes in the two corners - especially in the top right-hand corner - gives the impression that here the painting is unfinished. Rembrandt's much smaller *Ecce Homo* from 1634 (London, National Gallery) shows a similar background. The artist's biographer, Arnold Houbraken (1660-1719), described similar areas in Rembrandt's paintings as '...some parts were worked up in great detail, while the remainder was smeared as if by a coarse tarbrush, without consideration to the drawing...'.[46]

Portraits
The painting of the portraits, followed by the jackets and collars, formed the next step in the painting process. The detailed and carefully rendered portraits of the doctors suggest that they were painted after life. It is difficult to know, however, if Rembrandt sketched them directly on the canvas or whether the portraits were worked up after drawn sketches on paper or tablets.[47]

Rembrandt employed a slightly different painting technique for the portraits in the background than those in the foreground in order to enhance spatial depth in the painting. In the background we find smoother paint application, less pronounced modelling, while a cooler palette forces the figures to recede convincingly. In contrast, Rembrandt strongly modelled the faces of the figures in the foreground, in mostly lead white paint, using more lively brushwork and more pastose paint. Here the flesh tones are mostly blended, wet-into-wet, sometimes leaving vigorous short brushstrokes visible in more pastose paint (fig. 37). The sophisticated cool over warm transitions convincingly convey form.

<< 34. Cross section of the paint build-up from Jacob Block's eye socket. The thin brown layer seen in the middle, is the dead-colouring consisting of Cologne earth.

< 36. Cross section from the paint on Jacob Colevelt's face. The brownish sketch or dead colour in the shadows consists of Cologne earth, black and a trace of organic red.

The pigment combinations are subtle and effective: for the cool mid tones the main pigment lead white is mixed with small amount of red ochre, vermilion, black and a few particles of azurite. Although the variety of pigments available to Rembrandt was limited, he achieved an overwhelming number of colour nuances.

The bright-purple highlight on the cheekbone of Slabbraen, repeated less strongly in the face of De Wit, is surprising. The latter is one of the most brilliantly mastered faces by Rembrandt. In the combed back hair, light reflections were created by tiny curved scratches in the wet paint. In the strongly-lit forehead we find an unusual abundance of nuances in the flesh tones, varying from green earth, brownish-yellow over yellow and rose, red and purple, as if Rembrandt were testing the limits of his palette.

Corpse

It is generally thought that Rembrandt did not paint the corpse of Adriaen Adriaensz., alias Aris Kint, 'naar het leven', after life. There are no records of Rembrandt as an eyewitness to dissections, or of the corpse of Aris Kint being brought to his studio.[48] It is therefore intriguing that the hand of the corpse was first painted as a stump! This is evidenced on the x-radiograph, but surprisingly has never been mentioned (fig. 38). Whether Rembrandt recorded this detail from life or whether he merely blocked in the crude 'stump' form of the hand as an initial lay-in, is impossible to prove. When Kint was executed by hanging in January 1632, he had enjoyed a long career as a thief, repeatedly punished in Leiden, Amsterdam and Utrecht.[49] However, in none of the juridical archives examined was it mentioned that his right hand was missing or cut off. It would, however, be in keeping with seventeenth-century juridical practice in some instances to cut off extremities prior to capital punishment.[50]

68

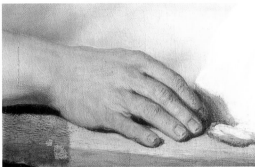

What we do know is that Rembrandt chose
to rework the initial stump form, covering it
with a meticulously painted, manicured hand,
certainly not that of a thief. Examination of the
hand and of the surrounding paint indicates that
the visual image of the hand and fingers is
integral to the painting, whereas in many places
the surrounding paint of the torso overlaps the
hand (fig. 39).

The parchment-like flesh of the corpse is
thickly painted in lead white with the addition of
a little lamp black, red and yellow ochre and a
little vermilion. The black gives a bluish tonality
to the skin of the dead thief (fig. 40), contrasting
strongly with the ruddy faces of the surgeons
surrounding him. The curly beard of the dead
man is accentuated by the familiar scoring into
the wet paint with a brush handle. The flesh of
the torso is modelled in almost dry paint, the
coarseness of the flesh suggested by squiggles and
dabs made using a dry brush in the nearly dry paint.

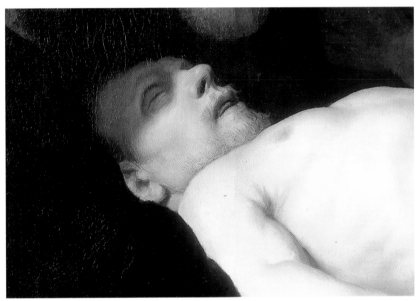

40. Aris Kint's head with
purple lips

Black and Purple Jackets

No doubt Rembrandt shifted to a new palette in order to paint the costumes of the eight gentlemen,
each of whom is painted in a slightly different hue and tonality. Each suit is rendered in varied tones
of cool and warm browns and blacks, and even purplish blacks. Despite archival references to the
repainting of Dr Tulp's jacket, cross sections indicated that the original paint is intact, although
covered in most places with overpaint (see also p. 60). The original build-up of the suit consists of
three paint layers over a very thin transparent brown undermodelling - here probably only a wash.
An opaque brownish black layer was applied first, which possibly corresponds to the working-up of
the dead-colouring, or to an evenly applied lay-in. This was followed by a very thick layer of bone
black, which also contains a tiny amount of red and yellow iron oxide pigment, and organic red,
which Rembrandt typically added to give warmth to the blacks. In some places a thin fluorescing
layer of lead white was seen in cross section, thought to be a thin grey highlight. The build-up is
quite thick, in the order of 150 microns.

41. Jacob de Wit's purple
jacket, which faded due to
the discolouration of
smalt in the paint layers.

42. Cross section of paint
from the same area.
Over a layer of organic
red, two top layers
containing smalt, a little
organic red, vermilion and
lead white were applied.

The build-up of the shadows in Calkoen's jacket is comparable to those in Tulp's jacket, including the brown undermodelling. Hartmansz's jacket, also painted over a brown undermodelling, is composed of a brown opaque layer over which a greyish scumble was applied, which serves to distance him from the figure in front, enhancing the illusion of depth. Furthest towards the back is Frans van Loenen, wearing a red-brown cape that was painted in a single layer directly on the grey ground. The eye-catching, purplish silk jacket of Jacob de Wit, who is leaning over the corpse, is composed of three layers of paint. The top two layers contain semi-transparent smalt, now discoloured, but which originally would have given the jacket a more purple-bluish tonality (figs 41 and 42).

Pentimenti and Final Adjustments

'The great number of pentimenti in the painting might easily be attributed to the lack of assurance of a young painter faced with a new theme as well as format,' Heckscher wrote in 1958.[52] This could be true if it was not so that also late Rembrandts often show an equal number of trial passages that have been repainted. The present impression of Rembrandt is that of an artist whose paintings evolved on the canvas, but under the restraint of a 'highly developed level of "management" in the use of colours and tools'.[53] The numerous small but significant adjustments indicate that the *Anatomy Lesson of Dr Nicolaes Tulp* also found its final form through an organic process until it finally satisfied the young Rembrandt (fig. 43).

'Two of the portrait busts (the one furthest to the left and the topmost one) appear not to be by Rembrandt, although they seem to have been added in his lifetime,' continued Heckscher.[54] De Vries, Tóth-Ubbens and Froentjes concluded that Frans van Loenen, the topmost figure, was part of the

43. Computer manipulation by Thijs Wolzak of the *Anatomy Lesson of Dr Nicolaes Tulp* Although we have no evidence supporting the theory that all the pentimenti were once undone simultaneously, this reconstruction of the individual original positions gives quite a different composition. Computer-manipulation by N. Middelkoop, T. Wolzak and J. Wadum.

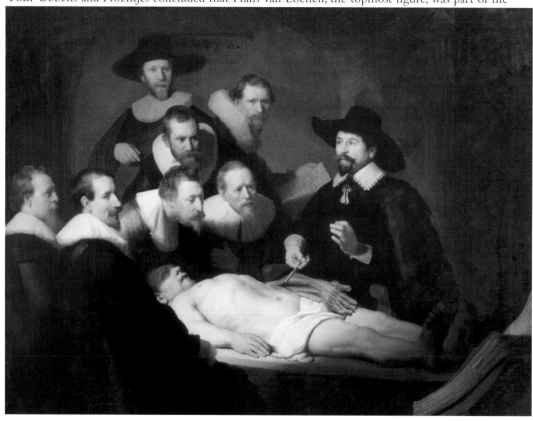

original composition, but suggested that Jacob Jansz. Colevelt was added over the background by another hand, possibly Jacob Backer.[55] In 1986 the Rembrandt Research Project correctly stated that all figures were part of the final composition conceived by Rembrandt, but stated that Colevelt was painted over the background at a late stage in the painting's evolution.[56]

The paint build-up of Colevelt, contradicting previous ideas, appears similar in build-up to that of the other figures. Over the grey ground, a brown dead-colouring was applied in the shadows while the lit areas were painted directly over the ground (see fig. 36).[57] In the contours around his face the brown sketch or dead-colouring was similar to that in the other figures indicating that space was left open for his head even in the initial stage. Elsewhere in the shadow areas the dead-colouring contained other pigments suggesting that it was applied later with a different palette.

The grey tonality of the face of Colevelt, previously explained by the idea of the figure being painted over the background, is in fact due to the thinness and unusual transparency of the lead white in the face. Furthermore, a multitude of small holes filled with darkened varnish (caused by the formation and subsequent loss of tiny inclusions) imparts a darker tonality (fig. 44). Also the loss of the warm pink light on the cheek makes the face appear flatter.

A minor but crucial change, as seen on the x-radiograph, was the repositioning of Hartman Hartmansz., the surgeon holding the anatomical drawing. A brown dead-colouring was found not only below his black suit but also in the background further up towards the left where he was initially positioned. The absence of the dead-colouring in the place where his hair would have been, suggests that Rembrandt shifted the head downwards towards the right without first making a detailed undermodelling. The brown layer visible in a cross section from Hartmansz's brightly-lit temple is inconsistent with the build-up found in the other figures where it is normally seen only in the shadow areas, though it may have represented the shadows around the left eye in the initial position of the figure.

A late change to the painting is the painting over of the large hat that Van Loenen is seen wearing on the x-radiograph. Cross sections show that the hat was fully finished in a dark brown paint, and that it was not sketched in in the dead-colouring stage, but probably conceived during the lay-in of the background. Rembrandt finally decided to paint over it at a later stage.[58] Dr Tulp then became the only figure wearing a hat, accentuating him as the *praelector*. This change, as well as the shifting of Hartmansz. to the lower position changed the initial pyramidal composition into a more coherent relationship between the portrayed doctors.[59]

There is no previous mention that Rembrandt originally positioned the head of Jacob Jansz. de Wit 10 to 15 cm diagonally upwards towards the left. Underneath the collar of Jacob Dielofse Block, a thick layer of pink flesh is seen in cross section. This is also seen on the x-radiograph as a faint whitish shadow (fig. 45). By shifting De Wit into the forefront, his head thrusting forward in a movement full of concentration on the lesson taking place, the composition is enlivened with a dynamic aspect.

44. Detail of the x-radiograph showing Jacob Colevelt and Adriaen Slabbraen. The difference in execution of the two faces is caused by a combination of technique and condition.

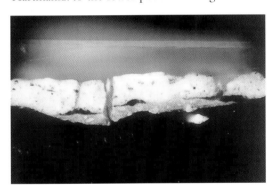

45. Cross section of the paint from Jacob Block's white collar. A pink flesh layer indicates that Jacob de Wit's face was initially painted here.

Spatial Illusion

Making paint on a flat support seem a tangible reality was the illusion seventeenth century artists were striving to attain. Rembrandt was known as an exceptional master in creating the illusion of space. The diagonal position of the corpse of Aris Kint is not only innovative but stresses how important spatial illusion was for Rembrandt in the *Anatomy Lesson of Dr Nicolaes Tulp.*

Spatial illusion is mainly achieved by the difference in painterly treatment of the figures as they recede into space, as discussed above (see p. 67). Rembrandt depicted the foreground faces in bright illumination. To successfully portray this, the paint was applied pastosely which invites a sparkle of natural light in the rugged surface of the paint. Plasticity was further heightened by various tricks such as scratching into the wet paint, as seen in the beard of the corpse and the hair of Jacob de Wit. According to Samuel van Hoogstraeten (1627-1678) the effect of purposely texturing paint enhances the *kenlijkheyt*, the perceptibility of things. He extensively described this in his *Inleyding tot de hooge schoole der schilderkonst* from 1678. As Van de Wetering pointed out, the following passage from Van Hoogstraeten is crucial to the understanding of Rembrandt's technique: 'I therefore maintain that perceptibility ['kenlijkheyt'] alone makes objects appear close at hand, and conversely that smoothness ['egaelheyt'] makes them withdraw, and I therefore desire that which appears in the foreground be painted roughly and briskly, and that which is to recede be painted more neatly and purely the further back it lies. Neither one colour nor another will make your work seem to advance or recede, but the perceptibility of the parts alone'.[60] François Desargues (1593-1662) writing about the *sterck en vlauw in kleuren*, the strong and weak colours,[61] explicitly warns painters only to employ strong colours like red in the foreground. By doing this one increases the effect of the area springing to the eye, thus enhancing depth. Certainly it seems that the young Rembrandt was aware of such effects. Red is found on the back and seat of the chair in the lower foreground, as well as on the dissected arm. Purple is used on the suit of De Wit, who leans over the corpse, which helps successfully place him in the space between the figures in the front and those behind.

The way Rembrandt painted the large book in the foreground is a wonderful example of Van Hoogstraten's notion of 'kenlijkheyt', or perceptibility. The shadows in the book are painted in brown earth colours. In order to simulate the tangibility and light reflection between the pages along the most forward edge of the book, Rembrandt scratched lines into the wet paint with the end of his brush. These scratched lines, nonchalantly made in a fraction of a second, underline the self-assurance of the young master. The brightly-lit pages of the book are underpainted with azurite-containing paint giving the paper a slightly bluish tonality. The text is not legible, and was never intended to be so, although, a capital 'R' appears to be the first letter on the page. This letter is comparable to what can be observed in the book in the *Portrait of Johannes Wtenbogaert* from 1632 (Amsterdam, Rijksmuseum). Similar scratched lines, alluding to crispness and detail in a book, are seen in one of the books in *Portrait of Cornelis Anslo and his Wife* from 1641 (Berlin, Gemäldegalerie).

The essence of Rembrandt's approach to spatial illusion can be found in the different ways in which the portraits were painted. The facial features of Frans van Loenen standing in the background are summarily and smoothly rendered with thin layers of paint that barely cover the grey ground, the luminosity of which creates a bluish mid tone around the eyes. In this way the figure recedes into the background as if something in the air hinders his readability. Van Hoogstraeten presents us with an explanation when he describes 'the thickness of air' *(de dickte der lucht)*, the presence of air between the viewer's eyes and the objects beheld.[62] Van Hoogstraeten is referring to the long established phenomenon known as aerial perspective, which manifests itself most clearly in landscape painting. In this we see that the landscape takes on an increasingly lighter, bluish hue the further it recedes into the distance, comparable with the decreasing intensity of the surgeons' jackets as one looks back in the composition. 'The thickness of air', so to speak, absorbs the intensity of the colours and produces a tonal difference with distance. In the *Anatomy Lesson of Dr Nicolaes Tulp* Rembrandt employed this painterly refinement, which together with the differentiation in thickness of the paint, gives the painting its special atmospheric effect. Contributing to this are the frequently adjusted and softened contours. The juxtaposition of angles between one form and another also allows for a smooth transition of space, almost alluding to a landscape with hills and mountains rising and falling into a hazy distance.

Glossary of Technical Terms

Cross section
A minuscule sample from the painting with a diameter of 0.03 to 0.06 mm. This is embedded in a block of cold-setting transparent resin, which is ground on one side to reveal a cross section of the paint layers. This can be analysed in reflected or ultraviolet light under the polarising microscope. Many pigments can be identified by their colour and optical properties and chemical analyses can be carried out on certain layers.

DTMS
Direct Temperature-resolved Mass Spectrometry: a fast fingerprint method suitable for identification of classes of compounds such as paints , resins, waxes, proteins, carbohydrates, certain pigments.

EDX
Energy-dispersive x-ray microanalysis: a method for the identification of inorganic elements in a compound (such as lead, copper , iron) either of a single particle or a whole layer. EDX is often used for pigment identification.

FTIR
Fourier transform infrared spectrometry: a method for the identification of organic compounds by matching infra-red radiation absorption bands with that of a reference sample.

GCMS
Gas chromatography-mass spectrometry: a frequently used analytical method for the separation (gas chromatography) and identification (mass spectrometry) of organic compounds, such as varnishes and binding media.

Py -TMAH GCMS
Pyrolysis gas chromatography/mass spectrometry in the presence of tetramethylammonium hydroxide (TMAH): sensitive method for small samples. Detects low concentrations and provides detailed information of organic components, such as degree of oxidation of di- and triterpenoid resins.

46. Petria Noble and Jørgen Wadum at work during the restauration of 1997-1998.

SEM
Scanning electron microscopy: a method where scattered electrons are collected, and via a video image the three-dimensional structure of the surface can be seen at magnifications up to 100,000x.

SEM-EDX
Elemental microanalysis of very tiny samples carried out in the scanning electron microscope (see EDX analysis).

Ultraviolet
radiating with ultraviolet (UV) causes different materials to fluoresce, which is helpful in determining later additions to a painting, identifying certain pigments and the nature of the varnish layer.

X-rays
long wave radiation passes through the various materials that compose a painting, their different radio absorbencies determining the resulting image on the film. The heavier the atoms of which a material is made, the more opaque it is to x-rays. Lead compounds

are particularly opaque and appear almost white on the x-ray image. X-radiographs are an important tool in assessing not only the condition but also pentimenti and pigment distribution.

XRD

x-ray diffraction analysis: a fingerprint method to identify the crystalline structure of inorganic compounds, including many pigments. Since different compounds possess unique crystalline structures the results are unambiguous.

Biography of Nicolaes Tulp

1593   Claes Pietersz. was born to Pieter Dircksz. and Gherytgen Dircksdr. in Amsterdam on 11 October 1593.

1611   He left for Leiden at the age of seventeen, and enrolled at the University as a student of medicine.

1614   Claes Pietersz. completed his study in three and a half years, after which he returned to his place of birth to establish himself as a doctor of medicine.

1621   On the death of one of his children in March, the burial register refers to a signboard with a tulip at his house on the Prinsengracht. This is the first mention of the name 'Tulp'. Two months later he moved into a house on the Keizersgracht, also with such a signboard. Upon his appointment as an alderman one year later, Claes Pietersz. needed a coat of arms for his seal of office. He chose a tulip. In the following years, the name 'Tulp' was increasingly used as his family name.

1622   In addition to being a doctor, Tulp was also very active in the town council of Amsterdam. As early as 1622 he was appointed alderman, a position he was re-elected to five times. Moreover, between 1622 and 1672, he sat on countless councils and was appointed burgomaster four times.

1628   Nicolaes Tulp was appointed *prelector anatomiae* (reader in anatomy) of the Surgeons' Guild, a position he would hold until 1653.

1632   Rembrandt paints the *Anatomy Lesson of Dr Nicolaes Tulp*. This may have been Tulp's second public lesson.

1636   In the beginning of the seventeenth century, Amsterdam's many apothecaries would prepare various medicines for the same diseases, as there was no manual with the correct proportions of ingredients. This desperate situation became all too pressing in 1635 when Amsterdam was ravaged by the plague and many died as a result of incorrectly prepared and administered medication. Tulp initiated the compilation of a large manual, the *Pharmacopoea Amstelredamensis*, with the correct doses, which he had probably already largely completed since it also appeared in 1636. Most of the prescriptions had a complex composition and contained more than twenty to forty ingredients. A *Collegium Medicum*, or Medical College, was established to ensure that the *Pharmacopoea Amstelredamensis* would be properly followed.

1641   Tulp's most impressive achievement in the area of medicine is undoubtedly his *Observationes Medicae*. He wrote it for his son Pieter, who also studied medicine and unfortunately died at a young age. The first edition (1641) consists of three books; Tulp added a

1. Nicolaes Eliasz. Pickenoy
Nicolaes Tulp, 1633
Amsterdam,
Six Collection

volume to the second edition (1652). Tulp translated this book, written in Latin, into Dutch, a few years before his death. The manuscript, which he called *Genees insighten* (see fig. 2 and *3)*, never appeared in print.

Tulp described his cases, 231 in all, extensively. He outlined the condition of his patients throughout their illness, as well as after their death when this led to a dissection. He was greatly interested in establishing his patients' cause of death. Among the diseases he studied were various forms of cancer and 'stones', a heart clot, heart palpitations, a head injury, 'loose skin' and a two-headed monster.

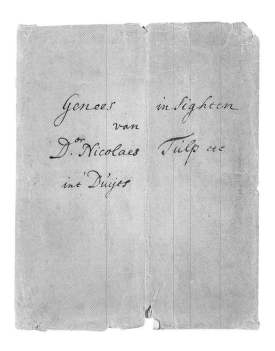

2. Frontpage of *Genees insighten van D.ᵒʳ Nicolaes Tulp etc int'D'uijts,* written after 1655 Amsterdam, Six Collection

We get a good image of Tulp as a conscientious medical man in an eight-page long description of the 'intestinal valve'. This valve, the so-called valvula ileocoecalis, had been discovered earlier by Caspar Bauhinus, but Tulp was the first to accurately describe and draw it (see fig. 4). According to the Doctor Vopiscus Fortunatus Plemp, who was always present at Tulp's anatomy lessons, Tulp demonstrated this valve in his lesson in 1632. This must have been the same anatomy lesson that Rembrandt painted.

That Tulp, as befitting a good doctor, was also an excellent psychologist is evident from the way in which he treated a 'weakling'. This was a 'renown painter', who thought that his bones were 'so soft, and supple', that he remained in bed the entire winter. In this instance Tulp relied on the placebo effect: for the sake of appearances he dispelled some black bile and assured the painter that if he obeyed the doctor, his bones would be strong again in three days, and he would even be able to walk on the street in six days.

For us, one of Tulp's most interesting conclusions has to do with the chapter on 'an attack of palsy'. He describes how a 'drunken youth' had died as a result of fall. In dissecting the body, Tulp discovered 'livid purple specks' on the lungs. He noted that these could have been caused by suffocation as a result of the fall, but also considers that the frequent 'smoking' of tobacco, to which this boy was 'mad about' could also have been the cause of the pulmonary condition.

3. Description of 'Een beroertheid' in *Genees insighten*, p. 15 Dr Nicolaes Tulp Amsterdam, Six Collection

4. Dr Nicolaes Tulp *Observationes medicae*, Valvula ileocoecalis (intestinal valve) Amsterdam, Six Collection

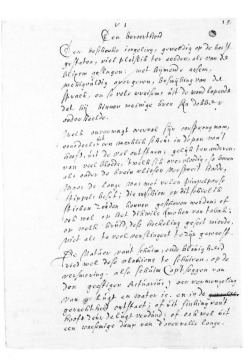

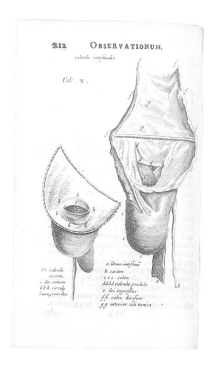

He delves further into this possibility, suggesting that the smoke be investigated: 'But there is the rub, whether the smoke is also a hindrance to the lungs? being a hot herb…'(in translation). It is striking that, regardless of the actual cause is of the specks in this case, he links his determination of their presence on the lungs with the frequent smoking of tobacco. In this he was way ahead of his time and may well be the first doctor to ever question the effects of tobacco on the lungs. Many other doctors assumed that inhaled smoke did not go to the lungs, but went directly to the brain turning it black, as was confirmed regularly during

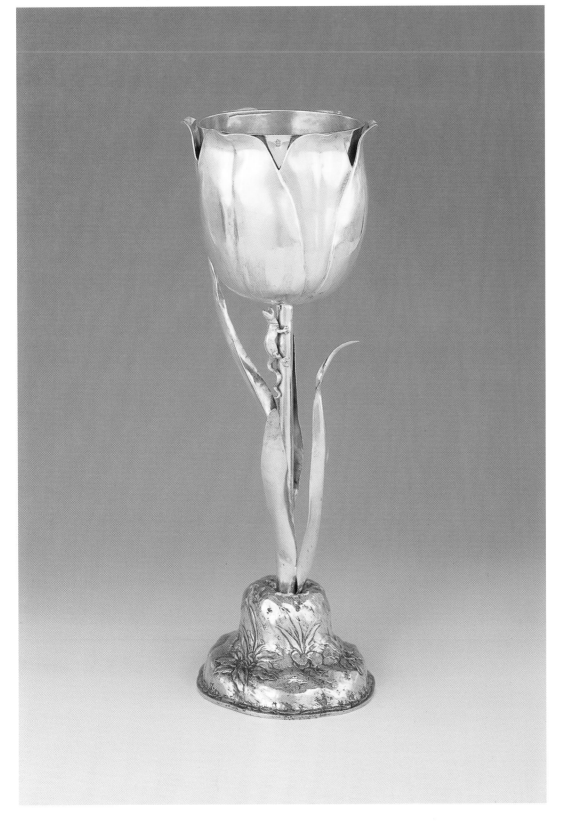

5. Johannes Lutma
(*c.* 1584–1669)
Tulp cup, 1652
Six Collection,
Amsterdam

dissections. It was thought that tobacco smoke could enter the brain via a hole between the nostril and the skull, thereby causing the black colour.

1650   After more than twenty years as a prelector, Tulp gave his last anatomy lesson. He lectured to the surgeons in training for another two years. However, it became increasingly difficult for him to combine this with his responsibilities as a town councillor.

1652   Tulp stops his medical practice.

1654   Tulp begins his first term of office as burgomaster of Amsterdam. He served in this office for the second and third time in 1656 and 1666, respectively.

1671   Tulp serves as burgomaster of Amsterdam for the fourth and last time.

1672   Tulp celebrates his fiftieth anniversary as a councillor.

1673   Appointed to the 'Gecommiteerde Raad' in The Hague.

1674   On 12 September, Tulp passes away in The Hague and is buried in the New Church in Amsterdam.

This chronology is derived from the biography of Tulp in *Nicolaes Tulp. Leven en werk van een Amsterdams geneesheer en magistraat*, published by Six Art Promotion bv in 1991. A revised English edition will appear on the occasion of the exhibition in the Mauritshuis.

1958, p. 115, makes a connection between the fact that Aris Kint came from Leiden, on the one hand, and the rivalry between Leiden University and the Athenaeum Illustre, founded in Amsterdam in 1632 and now the University of Amsterdam, on the other. *Van Eeghen 1969*, p. 4-5, queries this suggestion with the argument that Tulp had no connection with the Athenaeum, but she still describes Tulp's anatomy lesson as 'the crown on the Athenaeum's inaugural festivities'.

48. *Kellet 1959*, p. 152, suggests that Rembrandt's painting is not of Tulp's public anatomy lesson of 1632, using the body of Aris Kint, but 'one of the earliest representations of a private anatomy'.

49. *Monnikhoff 1750*, fol. 24-25. It is unusual here that the author gives no source. Even so, the passage appears to have been borrowed from a contemporary seventeenth-century source: 'In the year 1632 the aforesaid Paintings in the Guild Chamber were joined by that fine and excellent piece in which the renowned <u>Rembrandt</u> most artistically portrayed Dr Nicolaas Tulp, Mr Jacob Block, Hartman Hartmansz, Adriaan Slabbraan, Jacob de Witt, Mr Mathijs Kalkoen, Jacob Koolveld, Frans van Loenen.'

50. For the moment at which the names were added, *De Vries et al. 1978*, p. 99, suggests the restoration of 1732; Broos and Wadum mention the restorations by Pool and Blauwpot as possibilities. *Van Eeghen 1969*, p. 11, remarks that the list no longer uses patronymics but the surnames which those depicted would not start using until later on in their careers. The way in which the portraits are numbered, in small white numerals, is in some ways similar to that in the anatomy pieces of 1603, 1619 and 1728, but it is different from that in the paintings of 1670 and 1683. Numbers have not been used at all in the group portraits of 1684, 1699, 1706 and 1716, and there is no discernible numbering in the fragments of 1625 and 1656. It is possible that in 1632 Rembrandt was the first artist not to include a list of names as a standard component of the painting. For biographical information about the sitters, see *Van Eeghen 1969*, p. 7-11.

51. *De Naamen ...* (see n. 19), fol. 10; Jacob Jansz de Witt, the man bending over the head of the *subjectum*, became a warden in 1630 and an examiner in 1632; Adriaen Cornelisz Slabbraen, second from the left, followed the same career in the guild from 1631.

52. Barent Trist and Anthonij Testament had had themselves painted in 1625, Lambert Jacobsz in 1619; see n. 19 and 29. Albert Gerritsz Hop, like Trist an examiner in 1631-

1632, does not appear in any anatomy piece.

53. *De Naamen ...* (see n. 19), fol. 10; this was Hartman Hartmansz, the man with the paper (from 1635); Jacob Block, on the left next to Hartman Hartmansz (from 1638); Jacob Koolvelt, on the extreme left (from 1635); and Matthys Calkoen, at Tulp's right hand (from 1639). According to *Schupbach 1982*, p. 30 and 55, in 1632 Calkoen was Tulp's assistant. Frans van Loenen, the man in the background, never held a post on the governing board.

54. *Querido 1967*. *De Lint 1930*, p. 45, opined that the body's incorrect proportions could be explained by the fact that the dead man had been disfigured, the right side of his body being less developed than the left.

55. *Carpentier Alting/Waterbolk 1976* and *Carpentier Alting/Waterbolk 1978*; the authors give a summary of the debate up to that point.

56. *Hekscher 1958*, p. 65-76.

57. *Vesalius 1543*, Prefatio, fol. 1; *Hekscher 1958*, p. 73.

58. *Hekscher 1958*, p. 67.

59. *Kellet 1959*, p. 152 and *Querido 1967*, p. 135-136.

60. Cf. the *Two Scholars* (1628) in Melbourne, the *St Paul* in Nuremberg (*c.* 1629-30), *Johannes Uyttenbogaert* (1633) in the Rijksmuseum, and *Johannes Elison* (1634) in Boston; see also *Hekscher 1958*, p. 16-19.

61. *De Vries et al. 1978*, p. 82-113; see also *Corpus 1982-ff.*, vol. II (1986), p. 172-189.

62. See *De Vries et al. 1978*, p. 103 and 105, where Jacob Backer is suggested as the painter of Koolvelt's portrait.

63. *Schupbach 1982*, p. 6-7.

64. Ibid., p. 9-12 and 20-23.

65. Ibid., p. 21 and 31-40.

66. Ibid., p. 18-20.

67. Ibid., p. 22, 31-33, 48-49, 85-89; see n. 9 for the differences between the versions of 1639 and 1691.

68. Ibid., p. 41-44.

69. Ibid., p. 43-44. Rembrandt is supposed to have accentuated Van Loenen's leading role alongside that of Tulp by giving him a hat like the prelector; cf. *Hekscher 1958*, p. 118, who interprets the hat as a sign of rank.

70. *Schupbach 1982*, p. 28-29.

71. *Hekscher 1958*, p. 33-34.

72. Ibid., p. 120.

73. *Schupbach 1982*, p. 47-48.

74. Ibid., p. 35-41.

75. *Anatomieboek* (see n. 10), fol. 15.

76. See *Haver Droeze 1921*, esp. p. 3-7.

77. GAA, PA 366 / 213, *Oud Resolutieboek*, fol. 14; also in *Nuyens 1928*, p. 66-67.

78. *Anatomieboek* (see n. 10), fol. 18. Only two

public anatomy lessons by Jan Deijman are reported; see *Middelkoop 1994a*, p. 10-11. Conspicuous here is the mention by *Monnikhoff 1750*, fol. 10, of the anatomist Gerard Blasius, professor at the Athenaeum Illustre, in a row of prelectors who have been active on the guild's behalf.

79. What follows below on the subject of the *Anatomy Lesson of Dr Deijman* corresponds broadly to *Middelkoop 1994b*.

80. Examiner Dirk Visch, the wardens Claes Fruyt, Daniel Florianus, Laurens de Lange and Augustus Meijer, and the guild members Jacob Hernij and Barend Heems; *Monnikhoff 1750*, fol. 25. Barend Heems was to take his seat on the board in September 1656, at the same time as Calkoen, having been nominated the previous year. Jacob Hernij was nominated four times between 1655 and 1657 but never elected; *De Naamen ...* (see n. 19), fol. 16-17 and the list in *Monnikhoff 1750*.

81. Abraham Hondecoeter. See *Anatomieboek* (see n. 10), fol. 18; transcription in *Middelkoop 1994a*, p. 5.

82. Ibid., p. 26-28. The damage done to the painting by the fire of 1723 is referred to only by *Monnikhoff 1750*, fol. 25.

83. For Fonteijn's convictions see *Van Eeghen 1948*, p. 35-36 and GAA, *Rechterlijk archief* 5061 / *Confessieboeken* 311, fol. 14v-15r, 24r-30v, 34r-34v, 45r and 55r-56v; ibid. 5061 / *Justitieboeken* 582, fol. 114r-116r (with thanks to S.A.C. Dudok van Heel).

84. See *Middelkoop 1994a*, p. 5.

85. A Dutch edition of Vesalius describes the advantages thus: 'For when it has been taken off you will be able to handle it more easily and with less difficulty. Therefore the heads of beheaded persons are the most convenient of all: principally because they are only recently dead, though sometimes (which is very inconvenient for seeing the bloodvessels) they are almost wholly bled out, unless one has been able to obtain them immediately after the sentence was carried out. ... But if the head is still fixed to the body, place under the neck and occiput as many square stones, or a small block, as are needed to make the head lean forward and be lifted up as far as it would if it stood on its own base or support.' (*Van der Mauden 1646*, fol. 53-54); unfortunately the effects of the fire mean that it is difficult to see whether Rembrandt took this advice to heart.

86. *Hekscher 1958*, p. 70-71. For possible borrowings from the body shown foreshortened see *Middelkoop 1994a*, p. 13.

87. *Vesalius 1555*, fol. 755.

88. *Wolf-Heidegger/Cetto 1967*, p. 214-217, no.

128 (= fig. 13) and p. 240-242, nos 155-156.

89. *Schupbach 1982*, p. 40, says that it is unlikely, given changes in taste since 1632, that the painting was intended to serve a symbolic function.

90. Cf. *Tilanus 1865*, p. 20, n. 2. On the basis of Barlaeus's poem of 1639 both *Hekscher 1958*, p. 112 and *Hansen 1996a*, p. 31, suggest erroneously that Rembrandt's painting was hung in the anatomy theatre on the Nes; see n. 124 below.

91. *Fokkens 1662*, fol. 241.

92. *Dapper 1663*, fol. 450.

93. The painting is mentioned in GAA, PA 366 / 229, *Aantekeningen omtrent instrumenten, geraamten and beesten op de ontleedkamer …* (Notes pertaining to instruments, skeletons and animals in the dissecting room ...), *s.f.*, no. 26 and PA 366 / 294, *Aantekening van de instrumenten, geraamten and beesten op de ontleedkamer* (Note of the instruments, skeletons and animals in the dissecting room), fol. 10, no. 26: 'A Cranium painted by Hercules Zeegers and donated to the Surgeons' Board by Mr Jan Zeeu on the 5th of March Aᵒ 1663.' The first of the two sources gives some interesting additional information: 'NB the above cranium was painted from a skeleton given to the king of France and brought to him from a far-off land. The king then gave it to a gentleman who travelled with it and displayed it for money, during which it was seen by Hercules Segers and painted from the life' (My thanks to Jaap Wit for his assistance in transcribing the original Dutch). *Van Eeghen 1956*, p. 39-40, mentions the reference in the archives, though without the information added in 366 / 229. She also thinks that the Segers in question may be identical with a *Death's-head* by Rembrandt recorded in 1780 and 1853, though the dimensions are different; ibid., p. 36 and 39. From the documentation of a former owner of the painting it seems that the ascription to Segers has in the past been supported by Friedländer, Valentiner, Van Gelder, Hannema and Stechow. The possible link between the work and the Surgeons' Guild was observed by Van Gelder and Gerson (with thanks to Wouter Kloek and Alan Chong for this information and the photograph).

94. *Commelin 1665*, fol. 201.

95. Ibid., fol. 198.

96. See e.g. *Luyendijk-Elshout 1996-1997* and *Baljet 1997*, p. 39 and 45-46.

97. *Lindeboom 1972*, p. 69-71.

98. *Hansen 1996b*, p. 669-670.

99. *Anatomieboek* (see n. 10), fol. 20. Lessons outside the winter season took place in April

1668 (ibid., fol. 21), April 1673 (fol. 24), May 1679 (fol. 26), May 1684 (fol. 28), July 1709 (fol. 43) and April 1715 (fol. 45).

100. For the proceeds of this anatomy lesson see n. 11 above.

101. Blankert, in *Blankert/Ruurs 1975-1979*, p. 15-17, esp. p. 15, doubts the ascription to Adriaen Backer because of the comparatively poor condition of the canvas, calling the work 'probably a copy' after the original that would have been lost in the fire of 1723; alternatively it might be the original, much overpainted following the fire. This would account for the restorer having signed the work *A Backer K 1670*, the letter K meaning 'kopie'. Investigation has since shown that the surface of the paint has indeed been damaged, possibly as a result of heating, but even without this fact there is for the time being no reason to doubt the authenticity of the canvas.

102. The *Anatomieboek* (see n. 10), fol. 22, records Barent Heems (deacon and examiner) and Gillis Hondecoeter, Leendert Fruijt, Joris van Loon and Daniël Florianus (wardens) as being present; the board as thus constituted held office from [September] 1669 to 4 September 1670 (*De Naamen …* (see n. 19), fol. 20-21 and the list in *Monnikhoff 1750*). The portraits of Heems and Florianus appeared in Rembrandt's *Anatomy Lesson* of 1656; warden Thomas Ravens was absent from the dissection theatre and does not appear in the painting. However, the painting does include the surgeons Jacob Brand, Aert van Swieten and Rogier de Koen - not 'Rogier de K(ock)' as *Blankert 1975-1979*, p. 16, calls him. Brand and van Swieteren had been nominated as wardens on 4 September 1670 but only Brand was elected; see also *Monnikhoff 1750*, fol. 21 and 26, for the names of the sitters. The list of names in the painting - with a corresponding number next to each likeness - is incomplete, making precise identification impossible.

103. See *Wolf-Heidegger/Cetto 1967*, p. 214-217, no. 128, p. 220-222, nos 133-134 and p. 248, no. 168.

104. Another candidate proposed for the figure on the left is the Greek physician and anatomist Galen, whose theories Vesalius discussed; see *Blankert/Ruurs 1975-1979*, p. 17. *Hansen 1996a*, p. 35, points to a possible link between Apollo and the dissection in the picture: Ruysch's peeling back of the skin has a parallel in the story in which Apollo punishes Marsyas by flaying him alive.

105. *Van Eeghen 1956*, p. 36, suggests that the painting may be identical with the canvas trimmed at top and bottom in 1773 in

connection with the placing of the cabinet of Dr Jacob Hovius (now in the Vrolik Museum in Amsterdam [AMC]). However, there is no convincing evidence that the canvas was also shortened at the bottom.

106. See *Haak 1972*, p. 45.

107. *Hansen 1996b*, p. 665-666 and 675-676; see also *Hansen 1996a*, p. 100-116.

108. See *Hansen 1996b*, p. 675 and *Blankert/Ruurs 1975-1979*, p. 17.

109. See *Baljet 1997*, p. 37 and 45 no. 2.

110. In contrast to *Hansen 1996b*, p. 675, Blankert suggests in *Blankert/Ruurs 1975-1979*, p. 17 that the *subjectum* in the painting is not Pasquier Joris but a corpse prepared well in advance. However, it is very much to be doubted whether Backer would have worked from a corpse.

111. *Baljet 1997*, p. 39-40 and *Van Luyendijk-Elshout 1996-1997*, p. 55.

112. Ibid., 55-56.

113. For Van Neck see *Ekkart 1990*, p. 32-37. According to Ekkart, Van Neck's signature, *J V Neck / Contrarolleur / f.1683*, is a reference to his post as a tax farmer at Enkhuizen.

114. *Monnikhoff 1750*, fol. 26; *Blankert/Ruurs 1975-1979*, p. 219. *Hansen 1996b*, p. 666, expresses the erroneous view that the younger Ruysch must have been about 20 years old in 1683, and that there must therefore have been some deliberate reason for portraying him as a child.

115. *Wolf-Heidegger/Cetto 1967*, p. 317-318, believe that the representation of the child is borrowed from Veslingius's *Künstliche Zerlegung*, Leiden 1652, cap. 8, fig. 2, which contains a somewhat similar newborn infant with placenta.

116. Most of Ruysch's collection of specimens is now in the Kunstkamera in St Petersburg; see *Hansen 1996b*, p. 673, and *Van Luyendijk-Elshout 1996-1997*, p. 58-59.

117. See *Lindeboom 1972*, p. 108 and *Baljet 1997*, p. 39-43. *Hansen 1996b*, p. 666 and 675, points out the gigantic proportions of the child.

118. The *Anatomieboek* (see n. 10), fol. 27, mentions an anatomy lesson on 8 November 1682 and the five succeeding days and another on 20 February 1684 and the three days following.

119. See *Monnikhoff 1750*, fol. 26: Anthony van Paamburg, Abel Horst, Pieter Adriaensz, Andries Boekelman and Jean de Milly. They served on the board from 3 September 1682 to 2 September 1683 (*De Naamen …* [see n. 19]), fol. 25-26 and the list in *Monnikhoff 1750*). Pieter Muijser is absent but he had already had himself painted in the warden piece of 1679-1680 (fig. 23) (see below).

120. *Monnikhoff 1750*, fol. 26, refers to 1679 as the year in which the picture was painted; there is no mention of the painter. The sitters are Jan Koenerding, Pieter Muijser, Izaac Hartman, Gerret Verhul, Allardus Ciprianus and Govert Bidloo, who has been identified on the basis of a likeness to an engraving by Blooteling after De Lairesse; see *Blankert/Ruurs 1975-1979*, p. 199.

121. Blankert, in *Blankert/Ruurs 1975-1979*, p. 198-199, doubts the ascription to Maes and suggests Pieter van Anraadt as the painter. Although this would be Maes's only corporation piece, others see no reason to change the attribution; see esp. *Robinson 1996*, p. 37.

122. This composition of the guild's board corresponds to the situation from 7 September 1679 to 5 September 1680, except that Bidloo did not join the board until after 7 September 1679; see *De Naamen ...* (see n. 19), fol. 24-25 and the list of wardens in *Monnikhoff 1750*. The painting may not have been completed until some time in 1680 (see n. 124).

123. For Bidloo see e.g. *Lindeboom 1972*, p. 72-74. Bob Baljet kindly drew my attention to the doctoral thesis by W. Fasbinder, *Govert Bidloo en William Cowper*, University of Utrecht 1948, which refers to an argument between Bidloo and Ruysch, apparently dating back to Bidloo's Amsterdam period (p. 75-76).

124. My thanks to Jaap Wit for drawing my attention to the document; *Oud Resolutieboek* (see n. 77), fol. 30v-31r: 'To the Noble and Most Honourable Lords Burgomaster of the city of Amsterdam. The wardens of the Surgeons' Guild do hereby with due respect inform you that for seventy years now their guild chamber has from time to time been honoured with the portraits of the professors of Surgery who have in the course of time, by their outstanding study and great learning, given the surgeons most excellent instructions and have thereby been of great service to the common weal, for example the noble and most honourable lords burgomaster Doctor Sebastiaen Egbertsen and Doctor Niclaus Tulp, as well as Doctor Johan Fontijn, and Johan Deijman, and now Doctor Fredericus Ruijsch, which said gentlemen took their rank in succession for at least seventy years. Now it is the case that in the year 1680 Mr Jan Koenerdingh, Mr Govert Bidloo, Mr Gerret Verhul, Mr Pieter Muijser, Mr Allardus Ciprianus, and Mr Isack Hartman, being wardens, have had their portraits painted and have moved the painting of the lord burgomaster Sebastiaen Egbertsen, which

occupied the first place, to another corner, hanging their own portraits in its place whereas the present wardens maintained that it was not fitting to degrade the memory of such illustrious gentlemen by putting them in an inferior place. They [i.e. the petitioners] have accordingly come to the conclusion that he should be replaced in his former position, and the portraits of the abovenamed wardens put back in the place where they had placed the lord burgomaster Sebastiaen Egberts. However, as the present petitioners have received abuse from some of the said wardens about this matter, and are afraid that if they should serve in that position again they would make the same changes again, the present petitioners ask their noble and most honourable lords to order, in the margin hereof, that the portraits may retain such places as the above gentlemen from time to time and one after another chose them, and as may be noted by us in the guild chamber, and your petitioners will ever pray ... 'The above Petition we have placed in our Resolution Book on the 19th of February 1683. Deacon and examiner, wardens were / Mr Anthonij van Paemburgh / Mr Abel Horst / Mr Pieter Muijser / Mr Pieter Adriaensen / Mr Andries Boeckelman / Mr Jan de Millij.' The margin contains the note: 'Understood that the old paintings referred to herein shall be placed in the positions in which they previously hung, done on 22 December 1682 / signed N. Witsen / R in the 7th Grootmemoriael [great daybook] at the office of the secretary of the city of Amsterdam f 76 verso' (confirmed in GAA, 5023, *Grootmemoriaal / 7*, fol. 76v). For the composition of the board of the guild, see n. 119.

125. Judging by the similarity in the dimensions this can only refer to the anatomy piece of 1619, which, when it was completed, was placed against the chimney breast when the room was officially opened and thus 'occupied the first place'.

126. See *Van Regteren Altena 1950*: Rembrandt probably did the drawing to show how the painting was to be framed and hung; see also *Middelkoop 1994a*, p. 17-18.

127. See n. 120.

128. See n. 118; there is no evidence for a direct link with the *Willekeur* of 1682 relating to the midwives. It is unlikely that Ruysch taught them in the guild chamber where the painting would have been hung; see *Haver Droeze 1921*, appendix, p. XVI and *Baljet 1997*, p. 46.

129. The sitters are Jan Willink, Pieter Oosdorp and Gerret Corver (*Monnikhoff*

1750, fol. 26-27), wardens from 7 September 1684 to 5 September 1685 (*De Naamen ...* [see n. 19], fol. 26-27 and the list in *Monnikhoff 1750*); their names are written on the sheet on the left. The other wardens of the period, Andries Boeckelman, Anthonij van Paamburg and Jean de Milly, appear in Van Neck's anatomy piece of 1683; see n. 119.

130. For the construction of the *Theatrum Anatomicum* see e.g. *Nuyens 1928*, p. 72-76 and *Kurpershoek 1994*, p. 42-51.

131. Ibid., p. 44-47 and p. 83-88.

132. *Monnikhoff 1750*, fol. 27, names Cornelis Boekelman and Jan Six as the sitters; Boekelman served as warden from 10 September 1698 to 6 September 1701, Six from 10 September 1700 to September 1703 (*De Naamen ...* [see n. 19], fol. 34-37 and the list in *Monnikhoff 1750*). Despite the assertion of *Blankert/Ruurs 1975-1979*, p. 250, there is no reason to doubt the identification as Cornelis Boekelman. In other words, when the picture was painted in 1699 Boekelman was the only warden.

133. *Hansen 1996a*, p. 115.

134. Ibid., p. 108-116.

135. Their names are given in the painting but are difficult to read. *Monnikhoff 1750*, fol. 27, confirms their identity: Hendrik Smekes, Nicolaes Kies and Nicolaes Heems (from left to right) served together from 2 September 1706 (*De Naamen ...* [see n. 19], fol. 41 and the list in *Monnikhoff 1750*). Their fellow board members had already had their portraits painted: Abel Horst in 1683, Gerret Corver in 1684 and Cornelis Boekelman in 1699.

136. With the exception of warden Gerret Corver, whose portrait had been painted in 1684, the picture shows the whole of the board which held office from 5 September 1715 to 3 September 1716 (*De Naamen ...* [see n. 19], fol. 46-47, and the list of wardens in *Monnikhoff 1750*): Dirck Claes, Roelof Roelvink, Jan Koenerding, Hilling van Velsen and Benjamin van Tongeren (ibid., fol. 27, which gives the year as 1715; this may have been the year in which the painting was commissioned).

137. See also R. Ruurs in *Blankert/Ruurs 1975-1979*, p. 55.

138. *Notulenboek* (see n. 31), fol. 217 and *Monnikhoff 1750*, fol. 25.

139. *Middelkoop 1994a*, p. 22, gives a reconstruction of the layout of the guild chamber in 1723.

140. See p. 40, n. 14,17. It is not known when the Rembrandt was restored; see *Middelkoop 1994a*, p. 22 and 26-28.

141. Amsterdams Historisch Museum, inv. no.

A 7411; see *Haver Droeze 1921*, p. 33, *Niemeijer 1973*, p. 20-23, 206-208 and *Blankert/Ruurs 1975-1979*, p. 316-317, for the favourable reviews of the day.

142. *Nuyens 1928*, p. 79-81.

143. *Anatomieboek* (see n. 10), fol. 46. The last public anatomy lesson by Frederik Ruysch took place from 11 to 18 December 1723 (ibid., fol. 50).

144. *Niemeijer 1973*, p. 23-26, 209-210. The light entering from the right in the scene argues for the hypothesis that the Troost was placed on the partition separating the antechamber from the guild chamber to the left of the outside wall with the window; cf. *Middelkoop 1994a*, p. 22.

145. The sitters are Theodorus van Brederode, Antoni Milaan and Bernardus van Vijve, all wardens from 4 September 1727 to 4 September 1728 (*De Naamen ...* [see n. 19], fol. 52-53 and *Monnikhoff 1750*, fol. 27 and his list of wardens). The missing wardens were Benjamin van Tongeren, Roelof Roelvink and Jan Koenerding; see n. 136.

146. *Nieuw Resolutieboek* (see n. 31), fol. 79: Pieter Clevering van Vijven was appointed guild assistant on 28 June 1728 for a term of four years; the painting may date from after this.

147. See n. 153 and *Van Gool 1750-1751*, vol. II (1751), p. 244: 'The gentlemen are here seen at work and stand out against a bright background: dressed after the fashion of the day, wearing their hats, seated at a table on which a dead body is stretched out; each seems to be watching and listening to what is being shown and said with great concentration; the Professor performing the dissection is standing, with some instruments in his hand, in order to uncover the muscles and musculature, which he is about to identify. This is all so skilfully and naturally depicted in this scene that every artist and art-lover will regard it with acclamation, and it serves as no mean proof of the man's skill.' Van Gool adds: 'I cannot refrain from mentioning here that among many portraits with which this chamber is decorated a piece by REMBRANDT VAN RYN stands out, which along with many others is well worth seeing.'

148. The former guild chamber has a maximum height of 340 cm. In the scheme suggested in the drawing, the painting would have been about 315 cm high. In a poem written about the painting in 1732 it is described as hanging in the guild chamber; see n. 153 and *Blankert/Ruurs 1975-1979*, p. 319, based on *Tilanus 1865*, p. 32, n. 32.

149. Amsterdam, Rijksmuseum, inv. no. SK-C-87 (on loan from the City of Amsterdam).

150. Izaac Hartman, Adriaan Verduijn and Elias Huijzer (from left to right) served together from 7 September 1730 to 6 September 1731. Portraits of their colleagues Roelof Roelvink and Jan Koenerding were already in Boonen's warden piece of 1716 (see n. 136); the portrait of Anthoni Milaan, who evidently took the place of Dirk Smit on his death in 1729, is in the *Anatomy Lesson of Dr Willem Röell* (fig. 29; see n. 145); see also *Niemeijer 1973*, p. 26-28 and 210-211.

151. For this affair see *Van Nierop 1938*, p. 133-143, *Blankert/Ruurs 1975-1979*, p. 319-321 and *De Moulin 1988*, p. 168-171.

152. Verduijn and Huijzer, who had just taken up their posts as examiners on 6 September 1731, were removed, as were Roelof Roelvink, Jan Koenerding (Boonen, 1716) and Anthoni Milaan (Troost, 1728). The past wardens Theodorus van Brederode, Bernardus van Vijven (Troost, 1728) and Izaac Hartman (Troost, 1731) were declared ineligible for further nomination. Benjamin van Tongeren (Boonen, 1716) and Dirk Smit were already dead (*De Naamen ...* [see n. 19], fol. 57-58); see also *Van Nierop 1938*, p. 133 and 137. Pieter Clevering, who had been painted by Troost in 1728 and was the stepson of the disgraced van Vijven, would eventually resign; ibid., p. 139-140.

153. *Tilanus 1865*, p. 32, n. 32, quotes from a book of poetry entitled *Lauwerkransen* (Laurel Wreaths), published in about 1732; both poems refer to the *Anatomy Lesson of Dr Willem Röell*: 'To the painter Troost, for the artful piece painted by him in the Surgeons' Guild Chamber. Heir to Apelles, I see here the magnificent scene, your art defies nature and will stand the test of time, as Orpheus earned before; your brush, placed on the blue vault of the sparkling fires. Only had you painted the son of Asclepius would your fame rise higher. The rest do not deserve to have their pictures shine beside his, ignoramuses of art, unworthy to be praised: O, Painter TROOST, cover the rest of this scene, his likeness alone exalts your brush.' *Blankert/Ruurs 1975-1979*, p. 319-320, supposes wrongly that the second poem refers to the warden piece of 1731: 'To the cleverly painted piece by the famous Master TROOST in the surgeon's guild chamber, where it may be seen every Monday for two stivers. Wardenship was once given to astute men and most honourably accepted by them. They knew how to separate carefully the wheat from the chaff, their skill allowed them to see the nature of one and all. Then the

ground was set by art with certain pillars, now we see Pallas stand painted with three owls.'

154. *Notulenboek* (see n. 31), fol. 165; see also *Blankert/Ruurs 1975-1979*, p. 255.

155. According to *Monnikhoff 1750*, fol. 27-28, the sitters are: Abraham Titsingh, Wichard van Wesik, Willem Monnikhoff, Joannes de Bruijn, Cornelis van der Swed and Bartholomeus Vermij (from right to left), all of whom served together from 24 January to 4 September 1732 (*De Naamen ...* [see n. 19], fol. 58 and the list of names in *Monnikhoff 1750*; see n. 156).

156. *Notulenboek* (see n. 31), fol. 215: 'next to Professor W. Roell, who also wished to honour them in the said painting, with his portrait painted in a frame placed above the head of the deacon [A. Titsingh]. Next to the latter sits the first bookkeeper W. van Wesik, then, pointing, the first Petty Cashier W. Monnikhoff, then the second bookkeeper J. de Bruin, and next to him stands the youngest warden [C. van der Swed] who looks after our poor, and next to him the reverend chaplain, co-president and examiner B. Vermij. This painting cost the wardens approximately *f* 600 over and above what the professor paid Mr Quinkhard.'

157. See also p. 40, n. 17.

158. *Van Gool 1750-1751*, vol. II (1751), p. 132 and 244-245 and *Wagenaar 1760-1767*, vol. II (1765), p. 463; see also *Blankert/Ruurs 1975-1979*, p. 255 and 318.

159. *Blankert/Ruurs 1975-1979*, p. 253-254. Meijer is the surgeon who in 1736 published the *Privilegiën, willekeuren and ordonnantiën* of the guild (*Meijer 1736*).

160. From 5 September 1737 until 4 September 1738; apart from Meijer and Titsingh these were Jan Bekker and Johannes Lakeman (third and second from the right respectively). Following the death of warden Nicolaas Craanmeester (not depicted) on 10 March 1738, Leonard Coster and Augustinus Graver (both shown, extreme right and second from left respectively) were nominated for the post of warden; only Coster was elected (*De Naamen ...* [see n. 19], fol. 63). Finally the picture includes past warden Pieter Plaatman (extreme left); from the tax register for 1742 it is clear that he was one of the wealthiest surgeons (see *Van Nierop 1938*, p. 175). *Blankert/Ruurs 1975-1979*, p. 253-254.

161. The family coats of arms in the picture confirm the names given by *Monnikhoff 1750*, fol. 28: Hendrik van der Ven, Hendrik Sak, Otto Ruysch and Johannes van Gorssel, wardens from September 1743 till September

1744. The wardens for that year who are missing from the painting, Abraham Titsingh and Johannes Lakeman (*De Naamen ...* [n. 19], fol. 68-69), are both in the painting of 1738 (fig. 33), Titsingh also appearing in that of 1732 (fig. 32).

162. See *Punt 1983*, esp. p. 5; the publication preceded Albinus's better known *Tabulae sceleti et muscolorum corporis humani* of 1747, with illustrations by Jan Wandelaar; see also *Blankert/Ruurs 1975-1979*, p. 261.

163. See *Nuyens 1928*, p. 79-81, *Van Nierop 1938*, p. 141 and 145-146 and *De Moulin 1988*, p. 171. Relations deteriorated after Röell's appointment in 1730 to be inspector of the Medical Council, reaching a nadir in 1746 during a dispute about authority in matters of obstetrics; see *Haver Droeze 1921*, p. 103-106.

164. See n. 31 and 138.

165. Amsterdams Historisch Museum, inv. no. A 1480; *Haver Droeze 1921*, p. 33 and *Blankert/Ruurs 1975-1979*, p. 266.

166. For Camper see *De Moulin 1988*, p. 175-177.

167. *Nuyens 1928*, p. 83-86.

168. The persons depicted can be identified by the numbers next to their heads and the corresponding names on the paper lying on the table: Petrus Camper, Nicolaas van der Meulen, Loth Lothsz, Joannes Stijger, Pieter Jas, Abraham Richard, Coenraad Nelson and the guild assistant Gerrit van der Weert (from right to left); see also *Monnikhoff 1750*, fol. 28. With the exception of Stijger, the wardens named served together from 7 September 1757 until 7 September 1758; see GAA, PA 366 / 218, *Notulenboek 1744-1760* (after *Blankert/Ruurs 1975-1979*, p. 267): 'On Friday the 9th of June 1758 the painting that is to serve as a memorial for those who come after us was brought here to the guild chamber. It shows Professor Petrus Camper, Loth Lothz, Pieter Jas, Coenraad Nelson, Nicolaas van der Meulen and Abraham Richart, with guild assistant Gerrit van der Weert standing at the end. The picture was painted by the renowned Master Thibout Regters.' Since there is no mention of Joannes Stijger, standing in the middle at the back, his portrait was probably painted in later – possibly after his election on 17 March 1761 on the death of Coenraad Nelson.

169. The *Dedication of the Drawing Room of the Felix Meritis Society by Dr Andreas Bonn* by Adriaen de Lelie of 1792 (Rijksmuseum Amsterdam, inv. no. SK-C-1639, on loan from the Amsterdams Historisch Museum) cannot be counted as one of the anatomy lesson series as there is no lifeless *subjectum*,

the audience does not consist of surgeons and the painting was never owned by the guild; see *Blankert/Ruurs 1975-1979*, p. 175-178.

170. *Hansen 1996a* is the only serious author bold enough to draw conclusions about the Amsterdam anatomy pieces, but I believe that in places she is skating on thin ice. For example, she explains the existence of the anatomy pieces in Amsterdam and Delft in terms of a supposed inferiority complex vis-à-vis the university city of Leiden (ibid., p. 74): 'In contrast, doctors in the cities of Amsterdam and Delft were compelled to commission portraits that documented their participation in any lessons as a result of their uncertain status compared to their more established peers at the University of Leiden.' Here she is mistakenly assuming that the initiative for the painting of an *Anatomy Lesson* came purely from the prelector. In her conclusions – that 'these civic works displayed their [the doctors'] right of dissection' and that 'they demonstrated the skill and expertise of their portrayed sitters while simultaneously acknowledging the guild's authority' – she uses the competition between the University of Leiden and its Amsterdam equivalent, the Athenaeum Illustre, to make a forced link between the Athenaeum and the Surgeons' Guild, a craft institution which was entirely devoid of doctors.

While there is some truth in Hansen's observation (ibid., p. 68) that 'the paintings ... were created as personalized advertisements of prestige and status for their ambitious sitters', it could also be said to apply equally to portrait painting in general.

171. Hansen (ibid., p. 23) opines that 'the demand for, and importance of the anatomy lesson portrait itself, depended on the struggle for status of the medical professional in seventeenth-century Holland' and believes that this is connected with a 'rise and fall in popularity of the genre' between 1603 and 1773 (ibid., p. 22). Not only does she erroneously place Van der Laan's engraving (see fig. 25) in 1773, the year in which Jonas Zeuner based a reverse painting on glass (in the verre églomisé technique) on it (ibid., p. 139-140), she also overlooks the 'rise' of the warden piece after 1679 and the portrait tradition kept up by the members of the Surgeons' Guild.

Chapter II

★ Ben Broos wrote the text based on archival material, which Jørgen Wadum amplified with technical restoration commentary.

1. *Corpus 1982 ff., vol. III (1989)*, p. 172.
2. *Martin 1918*, p. 154-155.
3. *Marijnissen 1965*, vol. I, p. 2.
4. *Fokkens 1662*, p. 161 (p. 240-241).
5. Amsterdams Historisch Museum.
6. *Commelin 1693*, p. 651.
7. See also *Middelkoop 1994a*, p. 19 and 22, with an illustration of a plan of the guild chamber with an indication of the location of the paintings.
8. GAA, PA 366, no. 266 (NB: all of the sources mentioned in *Corpus 1982 ff.*, vol. III (1989), p. 187-188 and *De Vries et al. 1978*, p. 220-221, are here transcribed new).
9. The interpretation of the precise meaning of terms such as 'schoonmaken' (cleaning), 'herstellen' (restore), 'oppoetsen' (refurbish), etc. is virtually impossible as they are highly general in character.
10. *Te Marvelde 1989*, p. 63; *Van Nierop 1930*, p. 272.
11. GAA, PA 366, no. 266, July 1709, n.p.; 'Pieter Blaupot van A[msterdam], konstschilder' (Pieter Blaupot of Amsterdam, art painter) married in 1685 at the age of 30 (GAA, DTB, 19 January 1685)
12. *Von Uffenbach 1753-1754*, vol. III, p. 546.
13. Fragments from these documents were published earlier in *Geyl 1906*, p. 38-40.
14. GAA, PA 366, nr. 216, 9 May 1732, p. 182; first published in *Geyl 1906*, p. 40.
15. *Te Marvelde 1989*, p. 72; *Van Schendel & Mertens 1947*, p. 28.
16. Amsterdams Historisch Museum.
17. GAA, PA 366, nr. 216, 20 September 1732, p. 217 (NB: on page 165 it is stated that Quinkhard was to paint a portrait of the surgeons).
18. With thanks to M. Bijl and H. Kat of the Rijksmuseum in Amsterdam, who kindly provided us with the restoration report of 1994. The painting is now in the Amsterdams Historisch Museum.
19. GAA, PA 366, no. 218, 16 October 1747, p. 144
20. GAA, PA 366, no. 218, 6 June 1752, p. 377. On Van Dijk, see *Te Marvelde 1989*.
21. In that year he was paid for 'cleaning and improving the two mantlepieces in the sherrifs' courtroom; *Te Marvelde 1989*, p. 102 ff. Van Dijk received numerous commissions from the City of Amsterdam for 20 years, which would appear to indicate employment on a permanent basis; *Te Marvelde 1989*, p. 62.

22. *Te Marvelde 1989*, p. 79; *Van Dijk 1758*, p. 6-7.

23. *Te Marvelde 1989*, p. 82.

24. The concern for conserving paintings in a responsible fashion as well occurs sporadically in other writings. For instance, in 1750 Jan van Gool wrote that one should not use walnut oil but varnish to liven matt areas in paintings: '… no one is able, to so rub on the oil so dry and thin that when it is dry it runs together, and moreover no oil is known that does not yellow in time and spoil the paintings; also it can never be removed except with harsh solvents, which is exceedingly'; *Van Gool 1750-1751*, vol. I, p. 86.

25. *Wagenaar 1765*, p. 385

26. *Corpus 1982 ff.*, vol. III (1989), p. 176 and 182, fig. 3, supposes that this took place around 1700.

27. GAA, PA 366, no. 220, 31 July 1780.

28. *Van Biema 1896*, p. 561. See also note 40.

29. One of the earliest mentions of this occurs in 1660: '1660.- Invoice Morledt for Mr. Fouchot. In December 1660: A judgement of Paris affixed to a new canvas and overpainted … guilders 12-0 stuivers'; *Denucé 1930*, p. 59.

30. J.-P. Le Brun, founder and head of the restoration studio of the Musée National in Paris (now the Louvre), in 1794 described three methods for the consolidation of a poor canvas: 1) 'le rentoilage dit B la colle', the usual paste lining; 2) 'le rentoilage ou maroufflage au gras', a lining with lead white and linseed oil, or attaching it to a rigid support; and 3) 'l'envelage', transfering the paint layers to a new canvas; *Le Brun 1794*.

31. *Te Marvelde 1989*, p. 72: 'Lacquer, varnish and paint knowledge by an art lover' (1758), p. 79, no. 11

32. *Reynolds 1781*, p. 76-77.

33. GAA, PA 366, no. 297, n.p., 1796.

34. GAA, PA 366, 29 November 1808; *De Vries et al. 1978*, p. 220-221 (with no reference to the source). On Jan Spaan see *Bille 1961*, p. 58, n. 56,

35. ARA, BiZa, OK & W, 1815-1841, inv.nr. 4031, 26 June 1817; see also *Broos 1987*, p. 287, note 7.

36. GAA, PA 366, no. 297, n.p., 2 June 1817.

37. GAA, PA 366, 2 June 1817.

38. In the time of Hulswit's restoration, experiments were being conducted in Belgium on attaching flaked off paint. This was done with a solution of glue in water or with wax diluted with Venice terpentine in a bain-marie. The removal of varnish was considered risk-free should it be done with spirits of wine. The varnish was also often removed by rubbing fingers over the canvas, which effectively pulverised it.

39. GAA, AZ 1817, no. 2077. This draft is appended to the documents mentioned in n. 35; see also *Lunsingh Scheurleer 1956*, p. 30, n. 1.

40. *Van Biema 1896*, p. 561. According to S.A.C. Dudok van Heel, the original letetr has long been missing (verbal communication).

41. GAA, Financiën 1817, no. 1034, 14 May.

42. GAA, AZ 1828, no. 2182, 28 April; *Van Biema 1896*, p. 562; *Obreen 1888-1890*, p. 197 (Obreen published the history of the sale on the basis of documents in the archives of the Rijksmuseum and State Archives, BiZa).

43. Sale Amsterdam 1828, title plate.

44. Mauritshuis Archive, 13 May 1828, no. 353

45. GAA, PA 366, no. 297, n.p., 14 May 1828.

46. GAA, AZ 1828, no. 2650, 19 May 1828.

47. Rijksmuseum Archive; *Obreen 1888-1890*, p. 204-206, 17 June 1828.

48. *Obreen 1888-1890*, p. 204-206.

49. *Amsterdamsche Courant*, 19 July 1828, back page.

50. *Obreen 1888-1890*, p. 214-215.

51. *Amsterdamsche Courant*, 29 July 1828, 2nd page.

52. Supplementing the letters published by Obreen, reference is here made to the transcripts of the relevant archives of the Mauritshuis (22 July 1828, no. 359; 29 July 1828, no. 361; 31 July 1828, no. 362) and the transcripts GAA, AZ 1828, no. 2650, 8 and 9 July.

53. Mauritshuis Archive, 14 November 1828, no. 371; see also 21/23 November 1828, no. 373.

54. GAA, PA 366, no. 273, n.p.

55. *Obreen 1888-1890*, p. 243-244.

56. Collection catalogue Mauritshuis 1826-1830, vol. IV, p. 33-34 and fig. 100.

57. ARA, BiZa, 15 May 1841, inv. no. 4727; Mauritshuis Archive, 13 May 1841, no. 626; reply from the minister on 24 May 1841, no. 629.

58. Hopman is generally considered as the discoverer of the Dutch wax-resin lining method.

59. Between 28 June and 17 July, Hopman treated 298 paintings: all of the paintings in the cabinet were cleaned and 68 'opgewreven' (polished) …; 21 pieces were more or less 'afgebloemd' …; 11 pieces restored; 232 pieces more of less varnished …; The man worked at a rapid pace …'; A.B. de Vries in *The Hague 1967*, p. 51-84.

60. Collection catalogue Mauritshuis 1841, p. 15, no. 125.

61. Mauritshuis Archive, 31 July 1841, no. 639.

62. The varnish must have become very yellow by this time.

63. Mauritshuis Archive, 16 November 1845, no. 752.

64. *Van Leeuwen 1990*, p. 12-13.

65. Mauritshuis Archive, 5 June and 24 August 1850, nos 833-834; *Van Leeuwen 1990*, p. 13. The cleaning of the paintings did not necessarily mean treatment with Marseille soap, but could also consist of rubbing with Venice turpentine, an aromatic resin. These substances would penetrate the craquelure of the varnish and cause some saturation of the surface. To camouflage a possible uneven saturation a 'light varnish of mastic was applied to the dark or dull painting'. It is known that mastic, based on natural resin, discolours far more than the presently generally applied dammar varnish.

66. Mauritshuis Archive, 8 July 1846, no. 756.

67. *Ducamp 1868*, p. 49-50 (this text was first published in 1857).

68. Mauritshuis Archive, 29 June 1859, no. 974. See for Le Roy, *Thieme-Becker*, vol. 23, p. 116.

69. Mauritshuis Archive, 7 and 12 July 1859, no. 975 and 976.

70. Mauritshuis Archive, 6 August 1859, no. 977.

71. The treatment is not specified in this letter.

72. Mauritshuis Archive, 22 July 1860, no. 993.

73. Mauritshuis Archive, no inventory number.

74. Mauritshuis Archive, 17 September and 30 October 1860, nos 999 and 1006.

75. Mauritshuis Archive, 30 October 1860, no. 1007; thank you letter by Le Roy, 14 March 1861, no. 1014.

76. Mauritshuis Archive, 5 April 1866, no. 1146.

77. Mauritshuis Archive, 13 May 1868, no. 1270.

78. Mauritshuis Archive, 15 May 1868, no. 1271.

79. Mauritshuis Archive, 24 April and 16 June 1869, nos 1337 and 1357.

80. Mauritshuis Archive, 30 September 1932, no. C8.

81. As Hauser wrote in his only recently published notes of 1901, Hopman informed him of the wax-lining method; *Mandt 1995*, p. 215-231. From the correspondence between Bredius and Hauser it is clear that the latter in turn introduced Hopman to Pettenköfer's regeneration method. Furthermore, it is striking that Hopman published Pettenköfer's work of 1871 on the regeneration of paintings one year after the

first German publication in a Dutch-language edition with comments.

82. Mauritshuis Archive, 28 May 1877, no. 59.

83. Mauritshuis Archive, 6 June 1877, without inventory number.

84. Mauritshuis Archive, 27 June and 4 July 1877, nos 83 and 86.

85. Mauritshuis Archive, 6 July 1877, no. 89; see the appendices of 6, 8 and 13 July.

86. Mauritshuis Archive, 20 July 1877, no. 90.

87. Mauritshuis Archive, without inventory number; *De Vries et al 1978*, p. 106-107, figs 81-82.

88. Mauritshuis Archive, 31 July 1877, no. 95.

89. Mauritshuis Archive, 17 August 1877, no. 97 and 98.

90. Mauritshuis Archive, 23 August 1877, no. 100.

91. *De Nederlandsche Spectator*, 25 August 1877, p. 276.

92. See note 58.

93. *Mandt 1995*, p. 222.

94. In St. Petersburg and Moscow linings were done based on sturgeon-glue and honey.

95. Mauritshuis Archive, 5-6 April 1885, nos 28-29.

96. Mauritshuis Archive, 9 April 1885, no. 30 and 19 May 1885, no. 36. The annual report mentions by mistake 'verdoeken' (relining). Mauritshuis Archive, 15 March, 12 and 23 May and 6 June 1891, nos Ad 37, 40 bis, 43 and 48; Annual report 1891, p. 56.

97. Mauritshuis Archive, 9 April 1885, no. 30 and 19 May 1885, no. 36. The annual report mentions by mistake 'verdoeken' (relining). Mauritshuis Archive, 15 March, 12 and 23 May and 6 June 1891, nos Ad 37, 40 bis, 43 and 48; Annual report 1891, p. 56.

98. *Wadum et al 1994*.

99. Annual report 1908, p. 52-53.

100. Mauritshuis Archive, 30 May 1908, no. 303.

101. See *De Wild 1909*, who mainly rejects the use of copaïva balsem.

102. Martin is referring at the 1732 overpainting of Tulp's jacket.

103. *Martin 1918*, p. 131-132.

104. *De Vries et al. 1978*, p. 221.

105. Mauritshuis Archive, 23 February 1940, no. 1094.

106. Mauritshuis Archive, 15 October 1942, no. 318E.

107. Mauritshuis Archive, 19 October 1942, no. 318F.

108. RKD Archive, 11 September 1945.

109. Annual report 1946, p. 52.

110. Annual report 1951, p. 80-81.

Chapter III

★ We would like to thank the following persons for their assistance in analysing the results of the technical research: Karin Groen, coördination and reports (ICN); Muriel Geldof, microscopical research (ICN); Henk van Keulen, GCMS (ICN); Susan de Groot, FTIR (ICN); Peter Hallebeek, XRD (ICN); Sandra Kemp, SEM-EDX (DSM Research); Kees Mensch, SEM-EDX (Shell Research); Klaas Jan van den Berg, Py-TMAH-GCMS (Fom-Amolf); Ron Heeren (Fom-Amolf). The conservators took the samples and analysed the cross sections. We also would like to thank for their advice: Martin Bijl, David Bomford, Lesley Carlyle, Mireille te Marvelde, Alan Phenix and Ernst van de Wetering.

1. Paraffin was indicated by high amounts of alkanes with an even number of carbon atoms, DTMS, GCMS and Py-TMAH-GCMS analyses. Already from about 1900 paraffin appears in wax/resin recipes for lining and impregnation, though it was probably not commonly used until the 1920s;. *Schiessl 1987*, p. 168.

2. This was carried out either by D. de Wild, active in the 20s or by his son, A.M. de Wild, who was a restorer active between 1928 and 1950. It can also be seen that the upper left corner was treated locally, as well as the application of a patch on the back. Documentary evidence from 1942 alluded to problems of adhesion in the lining, and that a local treatment probably occurred in, or around 1942, by J.C. Traas.

3. In all varnish samples an oxidised triterpenoid varnish was identified. The very low intensity of m/z 143 in combination with the presence of moronic acid in a PY-TMAH-GCMS measurement indicates mastic varnish rather than dammar.

4. *Gombrich 1962*, p. 51-55.

5. *De Vries et al. 1978*, p. 108.

6. Oral communication from Ernst van de Wetering, November 1996. See also *Corpus 1982 ff.*, vol. III (1989), p. 174, 177.

7. GCMS analysis of the binding medium indicated poppy seed oil, a drying oil not normally identified in the paint media used by Rembrandt and his circle, see also *White et al. 1998*, p. 75.

8. White overpaint from the collar from Colevelt analysed with DTMS: palmitate /stearate ratios fall between the expected values for linseed oil (P/S: 2). Both lead and zinc indicated by SEM-EDX.

9. *Corpus 1982 ff.*, vol. III (1989), p. 182.

10. N.E. Pickenoy, the *Anatomy Lesson of*

Dr Sebastiaen Egbertsz. De Vrij (1619); the *Anatomy Lesson of Dr Johan Fonteyn* (1625) and Cornelis Troost, the *Anatomy Lesson of Dr Willem Röell* (1728). Kind information from Norbert Middelkoop.

11. *De Vries et al. 1978*, p. 89.

12. It is likely that the inclusions also contain soaps from other fatty acids.

13. The presence of red lead was established with the help of SEM-EDX.

14. Wadum & Noble, Poster: *New Aspects of 17th century Binding Medium: Rembrandt's Anatomy Lesson of Dr Tulp Examined*, Art & Chimie, International congress on contribution of chemistry to the works of art, Paris, 16-18 September, 1998.

15. *Van de Wetering 1997*, p. 132-152.

16. For a current overview of cleaning see *Hedley 1993* and *Phenix 1998*.

17. Varnish was slowly soluble in a mixture of isopropanol and iso-octane 1:1, and more quickly soluble in a mixture of ethanol and iso-octane 1:3; this mixture was used over most of the picture.

18. In cross-section it is seen that the oldest overpaint was applied after the completion of the painting by the fact that it runs into a crack in the original paint.

19. The reason that the older fillings were not removed in 1951- which according to the annual report from that year states they were - is probably due to their insolubility in commonly used solvents.

20. See *Wolbers 1990*.

21. In the signature the same pigments were used as in the background, with the addition of black pigment. This is comparable with other paintings from Rembrandt. Oral communication from K. Groen. See *De Vries et al. 1978* for discussion on the removal of a later overpainted signature.

22. A 15% solution in Shellsol A/ mineral spirits (with a combined aromatic content of 30%). See *De la Rie 1988*.

23. Modostuc, a proprietary filler containing chalk, kaolin, polyvinyl acetate and an acrylic ester; *Green/Seddon 1981*

24. President Light Body (Coltène), is a two component polyvinyl siloxane. See also *Renschke 1992*.

25. Here dry pigment and Winsor & Newton Oleopasto, an oil modified alkyd resin was used.

26. Mowilith 20, a polyvinyl acetate.

27. *Berger 1990*, p. 150-155.

28. *De la Rie/McGlinchey 1990*.

29. This work was carried out by the frame restorer Renée Velsink, Gouda.

30. *De Vries et al.1978* discussed the possibility of a horizontal seam, visible in a

photograph of the x-radiograph mosaic 12 cm above the middle of the canvas. *Corpus 1982 ff.*, vol. III (1989) rejected the idea of a seam in the painting, attributing the line to the difference in density of the lining material. In actuality, the line is due to photographing the x-ray mosaic on a light-screen with a horizontal join: thus a 'phantom seam'.

31. *Bomford et al. 1988; Groen 1997.*

32. The chemical elements were indicated with SEM-EDX. Red lead was also identified in the ground by XRD though it is probably a contaminant in the sample, since wet chemical tests were negative (3M HCL showed no dissolution of the red ground). *De Vries et al. 1978* described the first ground as 'yellow and red ochres, fairly homogeneous in character, with comparatively small grains of pigment. This ground has been mixed with a little white lead and a trace of chalk.'

33. XRD analysis of the grey ground indicated the following lead compounds: lead chloride hydroxide [Fiedlerite] $Pb_3C_{14}(OH)_2$, basic lead carbonate and neutral lead carbonate in the proportion: 20:60:20. *De Vries et al. 1978* p. 89-90 described the second ground as 'composed of white lead, chalk, carbon black, yellow ochre and umber ... and appears to contain a comparatively large quantity of binding medium'.

34. SEM-EDX and XRD demonstrated only a trace amount of chalk.

35. See *White/Kirby 1994; Groen 1997; Van de Wetering 1997* and *White/Pilc/Kirby 1998.*

36. Palmitate/stearate ratios fall between the expected ratios for linseed oil (GCMS). That it was not heat-bodied was demonstrated by Py-TMAH-GCMS.

37. De Mayerne graduated as a doctor in medicine in Montpellier in 1579, and moved to London in 1611. Here he became the court physician to King James I and later to Charles I; he was knighted in 1624. As a member of the court he met with prominent court painters of the time, including Peter Paul Rubens and Anthony van Dyck. This prompted his interest in painting techniques which he was later to write down.

38. *De Mayerne 1958*, p. 179-180, no. 89a.

39. *De Mayerne 1958*, p. 181, no. 92. We are grateful to Renate Woudhuysen-Keller who drew our attention to this recipe. See also *Keller 1973.*

40. The possibility that the red particles in the inclusion were the result of contamination by the red ground was eliminated. SEM-EDX analysis of the inclusions indicated only lead compounds giving no indication for Fe (red ochre). Red lead is also not present in the ground. That the drying quality of the oil was an important factor in the painting process for painters is attested by the numerous recipes from different countries.

41. *De Mayerne 1958*, p. 144, no. 23.

42. With the polarising microscope (1000x) it compares well with a sample of Cologne earth: the red-brown colour, the irregular rounded contours and form and size of the particles. Iron and chalk were detected in the EDX spectrum which supports this identification.

43. *De Vries et al. 1978*, p. 90 describes a mixture of Cologne earth and bone black. In the present study no phosphorous was found with SEM-EDX which excludes the presence of bone black.

44. *Ainsworth et al. 1982*, p. 27, n. 34.

45. See *Bomford/Brown/Roy 1988*, p. 74-79.

46. *Houbraken 1718-1721* (ed. 1753), part 1, p. 259. See also *Van de Wetering 1997*, p. 164.

47. *Van de Wetering 1997*, p. 46-73.

48. It is known that the Danish court painter Karel van Mander II (1608/1610-1670) was present at the anatomy lessons of the surgeon Thomas Bartholin. In 1653 he had the anatomised corpse of a woman brought to his studio to make sketches for anatomical prints. See *Povl 1971.*

49. See essay Middelkoop, n. 47.

50. Kind information from Dr Pieter Spierenburg, Amsterdam.

51. The brown dead-colouring is not present in the lit sleeve of Tulp's right arm proper.

52. *Heckscher 1958*, p. 123, n. 1.

53. *Van de Wetering 1997*, p. 150.

54. *Heckscher 1958*, p. 11, n. 1.

55. *De Vries et al. 1978*, p. 86, 105.

56. De *Corpus 1982 ff.*, vol. III (1989), p. 174, 182.

57. The dead-colouring differs slightly; in addition to Cologne earth it contains black and red pigments.

58. *De Vries et al. 1978*, p. 86.

59. *Corpus 1982 ff.*, vol. III (1989) considered the possibility of a similar change in regard to Van Loenen and Hartmansz.

60. *Van Hoogstraten 1678*, p. 306-309; *Van de Wetering 1997*, p. 179-190.

61. *Bosse/Desargues 1664*, p. 31-49.

62. *Van Hoogstraten 1678*, p. 306-309; *Van de Wetering 1997*, p. 187.

Bibliography

Ainsworth 1982	M. Ainsworth a.o., *Art and Autoradiography*, New York 1982
Alberdingk Thijm 1880	J. A[lberdingk] Th[ijm], *Schilderijen afkomstig van het aloude Chirurgijns-gild te Amsterdam*, Amsterdam 1880
Amsterdam 1993	G. Luijten, A. van Suchtelen, R. Baarsen. W. Kloek & M. Schapelhouman (red.), exh. cat. *Dawn of the Golden Age. Northern Netherlandish Art 1580-1620*, Amsterdam (Rijksmuseum) 1993
Van Andel 1981	M.A. van Andel, *Chirurgijns, vrije meesters, beunhazen en kwakzalvers. De Chirurgijnsgilden en de praktijk der heelkunde (1400-1800)*, The Hague 1981 (Amsterdam 1947)
Baljet 1997	B. Baljet, 'Frederik Ruysch (1638-1731): obstetrician, gynaecologist, and examiner of midwives', in: H.L. Houtzager and F.B. Lammes (eds.), *Obstetrics and Gynaecology in the Low Countries: A historical perspective*, Zeist 1997, p. 37-49
Baljet 1998	B. Baljet, 'The painted Amsterdam Anatomy Lessons: Emblematic or historical portraits?', *Proceedings of the 8th Congress of Curators of Museums of the History of Medical Sciences*, Lyon 1998, p. 54-69
Blankert/Ruurs 1975-1979	A. Blankert & R. Ruurs, *Amsterdams Historisch Museum, schilderijen daterend van voor 1800, voorlopige catalogus*, Amsterdam 1975-1979
Berger 1990	G. A. Berger, 'Inpainting using PVA medium' in *Cleaning, Retouching and Coatings, Preprints of the IIC Brussels Congress*, 1990, p. 150-155
Van Biema 1896	E. van Biema, 'De verhuizing van 'De anatomische les' naar Den Haag', *De Gids* (IVe serie) 14 (1896), p. 560-564
Bille 1961	C. Bille, *De tempel der kunst of het kabinet van den heer Braamcamp* (2 vols), Amsterdam 1961
Bomford et al. 1988-1989	D. Bomford, C. Brown & A. Roy, *Art in the Making: Rembrandt*, Londen (National Gallery) 1988
Broos 1987	B. Broos, *Meesterwerken in het Mauritshuis*, The Hague 1987
Corpus 1982 ff.	J. Bruyn, B. Haak, S.H. Levie, P.J.J. van Thiel and E. van de Wetering, *A Corpus of Rembrandt Paintings*, (3 vols) Dordrecht/Boston/Lancaster 1982 ff.
Carpentier Alting/Waterbolk 1976	M.P. Carpentier Alting and Tj.W. Waterbolk, 'Nieuw licht op de ontleedkundig fouten in Rembrandt's "Anatomische les van Dr. Nicolaes Tulp", *Nederlands Tijdschrift voor Geneeskunde* 120 (1976), p. 1900-1902
Carpentier Alting/Waterbolk 1978	M.P. Carpentier Alting and Tj.W. Waterbolk, 'Nieuw licht op de anatomie van de Anatomische les van Dr. Nicolaes Tulp', *Oud Holland* 92 (1978), p. 43-48
Commelin 1665	C. Commelin, *Beschryving der stadt Amsterdam*, Amsterdam 1665
Dapper 1663	O. Dapper, *Historische Beschryving der stadt Amsterdam...*, Amsterdam 1663
Denucé 1931	J. Denucé, *Kunstuitvoer in de 17e eeuw te Antwerpen. De Firma Forchoudt. Bronnen voor de Geschiedenis van de Vlaamsche Kunst I*, Antwerp, 1931
Ducamp 1868	M. Ducamp, *Les Musées de la Hollande*, Paris 1868
Van Eeghen 1948	I.H. van Eeghen, 'De anatomische lessen van Rembrandt', *Maandblad Amstelodamum* 35 (1948), p. 34-36
Van Eeghen 1956	I.H. van Eeghen, 'Een doodshoofd van Rembrandt bij het Amsterdamse chirurgijnsgilde?', *Oud Holland* 71 (1956), p. 35-40
Van Eeghen 1969	I.H. van Eeghen, 'Rembrandt en de mensenvilders', *Maandblad Amstelodamum* 56 (1969), p. 1-11
Ekkart 1990	R.E.O. Ekkart, *Portret van Enkhuizen in de gouden eeuw*, Zwolle/Enkhuizen 1990
Fokkens 1662	M. Fokkens, *Beschrijvinge Der wydt-vermaarde Koop-stadt Amsterdam*, Amsterdam 1662
Geyl 1906	P. Geyl, 'Kleine bijdragen tot de geschiedenis van de schilderijen van 't Amsterdamse chirurgijnsgild, o.a. van de Anatomische les van Rembrandt', *Oud Holland* 24 (1906), p. 38-40
Gombrich 1962	E.H. Gombrich, 'Variations on a theme from Pliny', *The Burlington Magazine* 104 (1962), p. 51-55
Van Gool 1750-1751	J. van Gool, *De Nieuwe Schouburg der Nederlantsche kunstschilders en schilderessen* (2 vols), The Hague 1750-1751
Green/Seddon 1981	J. Green and J. Seddon, 'A Study of Materials for Filling Losses in Easel Paintings, and their Receptiveness to Casting of Textures', in *ICOM Committee for Conservation, 6th Triennial Meeting*, Ottawa 1981
Groen 1997	K. Groen, 'Investigation of the Use of the Binding Medium by Rembrandt', *Zeitschrift für Kunsttechnologie und Konservierung* 2 (1997) p. 207-227
Guislain-Wittermann 1992	G. Guislain-Wittermann, and J. Folie, 'Former restorations and preliminary reports from 1627 to 1946', in *IRPA/KIK Bulletin* 24 (1992), p. 33-54
Haak 1972	B. Haak, *Regenten en regentessen, overlieden en chirurgijns. Amsterdamse groepsportretten van 1600 tot 1835*, Amsterdam 1972
Haarlem 1988	Exh. cat. *Schutters in Holland. Kracht en zenuwen van de stad*, Haarlem (Frans Halsmuseum) 1988

The Hague 1967	Th.H. Lunsingh Scheurleer a.o., *150 jaar Koninklijk Kabinet van Schilderijen, Koninklijke Bibliotheek, Koninklijk Penningkabinet*, The Hague 1967
Hansen 1996a	J.V. Hansen, *Galleries of Life and Death: The Anatomy Lesson in Dutch Art, 1603-1773* (diss. Stanford University), Ann Arbor 1996
Hansen 1996b	J.V. Hansen, 'Resurrecting Death: Anatomical Art in the Cabinet of Dr Fredrik Ruysch', *Art Bulletin* 78 (1996), p. 663-679
Haver Droeze 1921	J.J. Haver Droeze, *Het Collegium Medicum Amstelaedamense 1637-1798*, Haarlem 1921
Hedley 1993	G. Hedley, 'Long Lost Relations and New Found Relativities: Issues in the Cleaning of Paintings', in *Measured Opinions*, 1993, p. 172-178.
Hekscher 1958	W.S. Hekscher, *Rembrandt's 'Anatomy of Dr. Nicolaes Tulp': an iconological study*, New York 1958
Hoogstraten 1678	S. van Hoogstraten, *Inleyding tot de hooge schoole der schilderkonst*, Rotterdam 1678
Houbraken 1718-1721	A. Houbraken, *De groote schouburgh der Nederlantsche konstschilders en schilderessen* (3 vols), Amsterdam 1718-1721
Houtzager 1979	H.L. Houtzager, *Medicyns, Vroedwyfs en Chirurgijns. Schets van de gezondheidszorg in Delft en beschrijving van het Theatrum Anatomicum aldaar in de 16e en 17e eeuw*, Amsterdam 1979
Jensen Adams 1985	A. Jensen Adams, *The Paintings of Thomas de Keyser (1596/97-1667): A Study of Portraiture in Seventeenth-Century Amsterdam* (4 vols), (diss. Harvard University), Ann Arbor 1985
Kellet 1959	C.E. Kellet, 'The Anatomy Lesson of Dr. Tulp', *The Burlington Magazine* 101 (1959), p. 150-152
Kurpershoek 1994	E. Kurpershoek, *De Waag op de Nieuwmarkt*, Amsterdam 1994
Van Leeuwen 1990	R. van Leeuwen, 'De schoonmaakwoede van Mazel', *Mauritshuis Nieuwsbrief* 3 (1990), nos 3-4, p. 12-13
Lindeboom 1972	G.A. Lindeboom, *De geschiedenis van de medische wetenschap in Nederland*, Bussum 1972
De Lint 1930	J.G. de Lint, *Rembrandt*, The Hague [1930] (Great Painters and their Works as seen by a Doctor, vol. I)
Lunsingh Scheurleer 1956	Th.H. Lunsingh Scheurleer, 'Rembrandt en het Rijksmuseum', *Bulletin van het Rijksmuseum* 4 (1956), p. 27-41
Van Luyendijk-Elshout 1996-1997	A.M. van Luyendijk-Elshout, 'De moralistische betekenis van de verzamelingen van Frederik Ruysch. "Uyt de Klaauw kent men de Leeuw"', in R.E. Kistemaker and J. Driessen (eds.), exh. cat. *Peter de Grote in Holland*, Amsterdams Historisch Museum 1996-1997, p. 54-59
Mandt 1995	P. Mandt, 'Alois Hauser d. J. (1857-1919) und sein Manuskript über die Restauration von Gemälden', *Zeitschrift für Kunsttechnologie und Konservierung* 9 (1995)
Marijnissen 1965	R.H. Marijnissen, *Het beschadigde kunstwerk. Een onderzoek naar de mogelijkheden van een discipline inzake konservatie en restauratie* (3 vols), (diss.) Gent 1965
Martin 1918	W. Martin, *Alt-Holländische Bilder*, Berlin 1918
Te Marvelde 1989	M. te Marvelde, *Jan van Dijk, een achttiende eeuws kunstschilder en schilderijenrestaurator* (thesis), Amsterdam 1989
De Mayerne 1958	Th. Turquet de Mayerne, *Pictoria, sculptoria, tinctoria et quae subalternarum artium spectantia*, 1620-1646 (manuscript British Museum, Londen), ed. De Graaf, 1958
Meijer 1736	H. Meijer, *Privilegiën, willekeuren en ordonnantiën, betreffende het Collegium Chirurgicum Amstelodamense*, Amsterdam 1736
Middelkoop 1994a	N.E. Middelkoop, *De Anatomische les van Dr. Deijman*, Amsterdam 1994
Middelkoop 1994b	N.E. Middelkoop, 'Rembrandts Anatomische les van Dr. Deijman', *Nederlands Tijdschrift voor Geneeskunde* 138 (1994), p. 2614-2618
Monnikhoff 1750	J. Monnikhof, 'Na-Reeden', manuscript *c.* 1750 (see *Meyer 1736*) (Amsterdam, University library, ms. I C 33)
De Moulin 1988	D. de Moulin, *A History of Surgery*, Dordrecht 1988
Niemeijer 1973	J.W. Niemeijer, *Cornelis Troost, 1697-1750*, Assen 1973
Van Nierop 1930	L. van Nierop, 'Gegevens over de nijverheid van Amsterdam. Bijeen gelezen uit de advertenties in de Amsterdamse Courant 1667-1794', *Jaarboek van het Genootschap Amstelodamum* 27 (1930), p. 272
Van Nierop 1938	L. van Nierop, 'Het dagboek van Jacob Bicker Raye 1732-1772', *Jaarboek Amstelodamum* 35 (1938), p. 131-180
Nuyens 1928	B.W.Th. Nuyens, 'Het ontleedkundig onderwijs en de geschilderde anatomische lessen van het Chirurgijns Gilde te Amsterdam, in de jaren 1550 tot 1798', *Jaarverslag Koninklijk Oudheidkundig Genootschap* 1927, Amsterdam 1928, p. 45-90
Obreen 1888-1890	F.D.O. Obreen, 'Rembrandt's anatomische les van Prof. Nicolaes Tulp', *Archief voor Nederlandse kunstgeschiedenis,*. vol. VII, Rotterdam 1888-1890, p. 195-244
Phenix 1998	A. Phenix, 'The Science and Technology of the Cleaning of Pictures: Past, Present and Future', in *25 Years School of Conservation. The Jubilee Symposium Preprints 18-20 May, 1998,* Copenhagen 1998, p. 109-119
Povl 1971	E. Povl, *Kongelige porträtmalerei Danmark 1630-1682*, Copenhagen 1971
Punt 1983	H. Punt, *Bernard Siegfried Albinus (1697-1770). On 'Human Nature'. Anatomical and physiological ideas in eighteenth century Leiden*, Amsterdam 1983

90

Querido 1967   A. Querido, 'De Anatomie van de Anatomische les', *Oud Holland* 82 (1967), p. 128-136

Van Regteren Altena 1950   J.Q. van Regteren Altena, 'Retouches aan ons Rembrandt-beeld, 1: De zoogenaamde voorstudie voor de Anatomische les van Dr. Deyman', *Oud Holland* 65 (1950), p. 171-178

Reynolds 1781   J. Reynolds, 'A Journey to Flanders and Holland', 1781, in: *J. Reynolds, The Works*. Edited by Edmond Malone (2 vols), Hildesheim/New York 1971

Reznicek 1977   E.K.J. Reznicek, 'Opmerkingen bij Rembrandt', *Oud Holland* 91 (1977), p. 75-107

De la Rie 1988   R. de la Rie, *Stable Varnishes for Old Master Paintings*, 1988

De la Rie/McGlinchey 1990   R. de la Rie and X. McGlinchey, 'The effect of a Hindered Amine Light Stabilizer on the Aging of Dammar and Mastic Varnish in an Environment Free of Ultraviolet Light', in *Cleaning, Retouching and Coatings, Preprints of the IIC Brussels Congress*, 1990

Robinson 1996   W.W. Robinson, *The Early Works of Nicolaes Maes, 1653 to 1661* (2 vols), (diss. Harvard University), Cambridge (Mass) 1996

Rupp 1990   J. Rupp, 'Matters of Life and Death: The Social and Cultural Conditions of the Rise of Anatomical Theaters, with Special Reference to Seventeenth-Century Holland', *History of Science* 28 (1990), p. 263-287

Van Schendel/Mertens 1947   A. van Schendel and H.H. Mertens, 'De restauraties van Rembrandt's Nachtwacht', *Oud Holland* 62 (1947), p. 2-29

Schiessl 1987   U. Schiessl, 'Apage Satanas! Apage Copaiva!' Über Materialmoden in der Restauriergeschichte', *Kunsttechnologie und Konservierung* 1 (1978), p. 168.

Schupbach 1982   W. Schupbach, *The Paradox of Rembrandt's Anatomy of Dr. Tulp*, Londen 1982 (Medical History, Suppl. 2)

Schwartz 1984   G. Schwartz, *Rembrandt, zijn leven, zijn schilderijen*, Maarssen 1984

Van Thiel 1983   P.J.J. van Thiel, 'Werner Jacobsz. van den Valckert', *Oud Holland* 97 (1983), p. 128-195

Tilanus 1865   J.W.R. Tilanus, *Beschrijving der schilderijen afkomstig van het Chirurgijns-gild te Amsterdam. Met eenige historische aanteekeningen omtrent het gild, en eene nadere beschouwing der kunstwaarde der verzameling*, Amsterdam 1865 [the last part is written by J. Gosschalk]

Tulp 1991   T. Beijer, H.A. Bosman-Jelgersma, S.A.C. Dudok van Heel, J.N. Keeman, G. Nolthenius de Man, I.C.E. Wesdorp, *Nicolaes Tulp, Leven en werk van een Amsterdams geneesheer en magistraat*, Amsterdam 1991

Von Uffenbach 1753-1754   Z.C. von Uffenbach, *Merkwürdige Reisen durch Niedersachsen, Holland und England* (3 vols), Frankfurt/Leipzig 1753-1754

Vesalius 1543   Andreas Vesalius, *De humani corporis fabrica libri septem*, Basle 1543

Vesalius 1555   Andreas Vesalius, *De humani corporis fabrica libri septem*, Basle 1555[2]

De Vries et al. 1978   A.B. de Vries, M. Tóth-Ubbens and W. Froentjes, *Rembrandt in the Mauritshuis: an interdisciplinary study*, Alphen aan den Rijn 1978

Wadum et al. 1994   J. Wadum, R. Hoppenbrouwer and L. Struick van der Loeff, *Vermeer in het licht. Verslag van de restauratie van het 'Gezicht op Delft' en het 'Meisje met de parel' van Johannes Vermeer*, The Hague 1994

Wagenaar 1760-1767   J. Wagenaar, *Amsterdam in zyne opkomst, aanwas, geschiedenissen, voor regten, koophandel, gebouwen, kerkenstaat, scholen, schutterije, gilden en regeeringe...* (3 vols), Amsterdam 1760-1767

Van de Wetering 1997   E. van de Wetering, *Rembrandt: The Painter at Work*, Amsterdam 1997

White/Kirby 1994   R. White and J. Kirby, 'Rembrandt and his Circle: Seventeenth-Century Dutch Paint Media Re-examined', in *National Gallery Technical Bulletin* 15 (1994), p. 64-78

White et al. 1998   R. White, J. Pilc and J. Kirby, 'Analysis of Paint Media', in *National Gallery Technical Bulletin* 19 (1998), p. 74-95

De Wild 1909   C.F.L. de Wild, 'Iets over copaivabalsem als schilderijenvernis', *Bulletin van den Nederlandse Oudheidkundige Bond* 2 (1909), no. 2, p. 42-46

Wolbers 1990   R.C. Wolbers, *New Methods in the Cleaning of Paintings*, The Getty Conservation Institute, Malibu 1990

Wolf-Heidegger/Cetto 1967   G. Wolf-Heidegger and A.M. Cetto, *Die anatomische Sektion in bildlicher Darstellung*, Basle/New York 1967

Colophon

Translation
Harry Lake, Bussum (essay Middelkoop)
Kist & Kilian, Amsterdam (essay Broos/Wadum)
Heleen Heckman, Leiden (final check of essay Noble/Wadum)

Editing
Marlies Enklaar and Peter van der Ploeg

Photography
Ed Brandon, The Hague (*The Anatomy Lesson of Dr Nicolaes Tulp* before, during and after restoration)
Wiebe Kiestra, The Hague (the restoration in progress, opposite Preface)
Technical photography and spectra in essay Noble & Wadum
K. Groen (fig. 7), S. de Groot (figs 16 and 33) and S. Kemp (fig. 31)

Design and Production
Six Art Promotion b.v., Amsterdam